The Canary Islands

The Canary Islands

HENRY MYHILL

FABER AND FABER LIMITED
3 QUEEN SQUARE
LONDON

First published in 1968
by Faber and Faber Limited
3 Queen Square London W.C.1.
Reprinted in 1970
First published in this edition 1972
All rights reserved
Printed in Great Britain
by Straker Brothers Ltd, Whitstable

ISBN 0 571 10122 4

To my Mother
remembering three happy winters
in the Canaries

Contents

Appendices

7

Maps

Illustrations

Illustrations

Acknowledgements

I wish to thank the Librarians of La Laguna University for giving me the freedom of their Canary section for day after day during the spring of 1966 and again during the spring of 1971.

Following the publication of the 1968 edition, Professor P. E. Russell of Oxford University made constructive criticisms of certain historical sections of the text. I am most grateful for these, and have endeavoured to alter these sections on the lines suggested by him.

I am grateful to the following people and agencies for permission to use their photographs:

Plates 1, 3, 22: Spanish National Tourist Office, London S.W.1.

Plates 2, 4, 5, 6, 7, 8: Mr. Michael Wright of Faber and Faber Ltd

Plates 9, 10, 14, 15, 16, 17, 18, 19, 20: Ediciones Sicilia, Jesús 2, Zaragoza, Spain.

Plates 11, 12, 13: Gregers Nielsen, Delta Photos, 8 Asgaardsdej, Copenhagen V, Denmark.

Plates 23, 24: Foto 'Raman', San Sebastián de la Gomera, Canary Islands

Plates 25, 26: Sr. Don Ramón Ayala Alamo, Valverde, Hierro, Canary Islands.

Plates 27, 28, 29, 30, 31: Sr. Don Miguel Bethencourt Arrocha, Santa Cruz de la Palma, Canary Islands.

Plates 32, 33: Ediciones Arribas, Paseo Ruiseñores 35, Zaragoza, Spain.

Plate 34: Trabajos Fotográficos Aéreos, S.A., Avenida de América 47, Madrid, Spain.

Individual Spanish words have all been placed in italics, with the exceptions of fiesta, patio, cordillera, conquistador and Guanche.

The nomenclature adopted for the islands, although illogical, is the one least likely to confuse, for it is the one spontaneously adopted by visitors who have been in the islands for more than a week and less than a year. Lanzarote, Fuerteventura and La Palma have no English forms and present no problem. Grand Canary and Teneriffe, although hallowed by long usage, are meaningless in the islands themselves. As they could not in any case be employed consistently throughout the book, I have substituted the Spanish forms Gran Canaria and Tenerife. But although foreigners soon learn to talk about La Palma, they have the greatest difficulty in referring to the other two western islands as La Gomera and El Hierro. So for these I have retained the simplified English forms, without the article.

1

Going South

April may be the cruellest month, but throughout Europe November is the most depressing. Whether or not October generously bestows a brief St. Martin's summer, it at least never fails to turn the great kaleidoscope of autumn colours. But in November the trees are bare. Even down on the Mediterranean they have given up hoping for a last out-of-season heat-wave. Did you order the fuel? Have you seen to the central-heating repairs? Do you need a new overcoat? Is the radiator of your car filled with anti-freeze?

Or are you going south?

To be going south you must be lucky enough to have a little money in the bank, and no commitments to keep you at home. Quite large numbers of people have that amount of luck, yet few go south.

Some are lucky and unaware of the fact. They simply stay at home, amidst the fogs of England or the snows of Scandinavia.

Some are lucky and fashionable. They make for Cannes or St. Moritz.

Some are lucky and rich. They depart to the West Indies.

Only those who are intelligent as well as lucky go south. That is all they have in common: a little good fortune, added to enough common sense to put it to the best use. Let us look at some of them as they set off.

Mr. Brown is a fat-stock farmer in the south of England. He has not farmed all his life. He was an engineer until a take-over bid left him with a golden handshake and fifteen years of active life to fill. Perhaps for this reason he approached agriculture with a fresh outlook. Mrs. Brown, however, is a farmer's daughter, so that their farm is run on sound lines, although not on lines which her father would have approved. They stick to fattening cattle, which they purchase in the spring and sell before Christmas. And in the unoccupied interval they go south.

They travel from Southampton, which is near their home, on the Spanish Trasatlántica line. They enjoy meeting interesting people travelling to Venezuela and Mexico, and the time spent in harbour at Corunna or Vigo in north-west Spain. Then they leave the ship at its last port of call on this side of the Atlantic, at Tenerife, largest of the Canary Islands.

Mr. Nuttall is retired and a widower. When his wife died he sold up his home and took a service flat in London, where he could see his married children. But after spending Christmas with them he never outstays his welcome. Instead he goes south.

He travels on one of the Aznar Line's ships from London Bridge, celebrating the new year as he sails down the Channel. Before the first week of January is out he is established in another service flat at Las Palmas, the largest city of the Canary Islands.

Monsieur Dupont did well in far-eastern trade in the days when Indo-China meant little to European ears, and Vietnam meant nothing. Like every good Frenchman he's glad to be home. But winter in his pleasant house near Tours is too cold for blood thinned by twenty years in Saigon. So every autumn he and his wife go south.

They drive their Citroen DS to Barcelona, trailing a comfortable caravan, and embark on a ship of the Trasmediterranea Line. Four days later car and caravan are swung ashore at Santa Cruz de Tenerife, and M. and Mme. Dupont drive to a secluded cove with safe swimming. There they are later joined by three other couples from various corners of France, old Indo-China hands like themselves, who over many a good dinner relive with them the *belle époque* of old Annam.

Going South

Kristina Lafquist is a painter, who in recent years has built up a small but quality following in Stockholm and Copenhagen. Like more artists than is generally allowed she is a good business-woman, and has learnt not to saturate her particular market. Her single exhibition each year, soon after Walpurgis-night, marks her personal reappearance in the Scandinavian art world, and coincides with the opening of the brief Nordic summer.

She returns to Sweden on the last of the cheap charter flights from Las Palmas. And as soon as these recommence, when in the autumn the Scandinavian air fleets are switched from the Medi-terranean routes to the Canaries, Kristina Lafquist goes south.

Franz Glück works all summer for a German travel agency in Italy. Early in October when the season ends he drives his Volks-wagen back across the Alps for a few weeks at home. Then, neatly packing his tiny tent, his inflatable canoe, and his equipment for underwater fishing, he heads across the Rhine and goes south, down the Rhone valley.

Some twenty-five kilometres beyond Montélimar a sign tells him that he is entering the department of Vaucluse, which draws its name from that fountain of Vaucluse where Petrarch, the poet who so inspired him in his student days at Heidelberg, himself drew inspiration. He is back in Provence, where the sunshine is still more than a memory.

At Avignon he parks his car beneath the Palais des Papes, and eats his picnic lunch in the gardens which command the view across to Villeneuve beyond the famous ruined bridge. And he imagines the scene described by Petrarch which was enacted on this very spot more than six hundred years ago; when Clement VI, with all the pomp an exiled Pope could muster, proclaimed Luis de la Cerda, the Count of Clermont, as Prince of Fortune.

Thus the grandson of Alfonso the Wise of Castile, and great-grandson of St. Louis of France, secured a kingdom of his own, a kingdom still to conquer, a kingdom of islands which had barely emerged from a long millennium of oblivion. So indefinite was their position that Edward III of England withdrew his ambassador from Avignon on the grounds that the Fortunate Islands in the

Going South

Atlantic so gaily bestowed by the Vicar of Christ were none other than the islands of his own damp and cloudy realm. And the nearest that poor Luis de la Cerda ever got to any Fortunate Islands was when he died fighting the English at the battle of Crécy.

Franz is luckier. He already knows the Fortunate Islands, and in a week from now he will be setting up his tent beside a lonely beach on his own favourite island, Fuerteventura. He is luckier, too, here in Avignon. For on that day in December, 1344, so Petrarch tells us, the brilliant celebrations were ruined by a violent rainstorm, which drove the Prince of Fortune to take shelter in his inn. But today the sky is clear and the Mistral is stilled. In Montpellier or Perpignan the weather may not be so good, so Franz decides to seize the opportunity of buying a few books.

For only at the University city of La Laguna in Tenerife will the visitor to the Canary Islands find a good bookshop;[1] and in Fuerteventura good books are even scarcer than drinking water. Don Miguel Unamuno, when exiled to Fuerteventura forty years ago, therefore carried with him an austere but comprehensive library of three volumes: *The Divine Comedy* of Dante, the *Poems* of Leopardi, and the New Testament. In admiration of his predecessor and grateful for his evident love of Italian literature, Franz has these same three volumes in his luggage. But he has room for a more widespread selection, and presently emerges from a bookshop with a dozen *Livres de Poche*. Over the winter evenings ahead, as his contemporaries in Hamburg and Stuttgart watch television, he will be reading Rabelais on Jandía.

For three months of the second winter after her husband died Madame Neuve was confined by bronchitis within her apartment in Brussels. Between bouts of coughing she gazed out at the grey fog. Even in good health she felt lonely. They had always moved in a society of married couples who now found no place for an odd widow at their cosy dinner parties and out-of-town luncheons. Rising prices were hitting her just as a large part of her husband's pension had ceased at his death. So as the third autumn drew in she let her flat at a high rental to one of the Common Market

[1] Las Palmas, Santa Cruz de Tenerife, and Peuto de la Cruz.

Eurocrats who were just then moving into Brussels, and went south.

Life in the sunshine suited her so well that she never came north again, except for a brief annual visit to collect a fat cheque from her lawyer and to enjoy the envy of some of her former friends, now widowed like herself and suffering the financial worries from which she had escaped. To begin with she moved around Andalusia and the Algarve, until during an unusually cold January one of the many friends she made so easily at cafés or on the beach told her about the Canaries. And now each November she takes the Trasmediterranea line's ship from Seville, sailing past the Golden Tower down the Guadalquivir by the same romantic route taken by the galleons of the Indies, when the Canaries formed the essential staging post on the voyage to the Spanish Main.

The Canaries are small only by comparison with the African continent off which they lie, and of which geographically they form part. Their million inhabitants are spread unequally over seven islands which together cover more than 2,800 square miles, and sprawl across nearly four hundred miles of the north Atlantic. We might expect, therefore, that our eight typical visitors will be lost to view as soon as they land, and are unlikely ever to see one another.

One of the most curious and pleasant features, however, of making a prolonged visit to these islands is that one seems to meet and to meet again everyone else who is doing the same. Not only will all our eight visitors bump into each other this winter, on boats, in banks, on beaches, or at bars, but we, too, if we go south, will make their acquaintance in circumstances which appear now coincidental, now almost surrealist.

I have myself caught sight of Mr. and Mrs. Brown after two years without hearing their names mentioned, their faces picked out by a naked electric bulb in a simple open air café of the fishing village of Los Cristianos in southern Tenerife.

I have suddenly recognized a profile at the window of a *guagua* (a word to learn before we go any further: it is pronounced *wow-wow* and it means a bus) hastening past me at Las Palmas as that of

Mr. Nuttall, whom I had met when he landed some months earlier from the same ship as one of my relatives.

I had often exchanged a brief word with the Duponts when staying near their secluded cove. But it came as a shock one windy and moonless night as I drove my motor caravan to a field near La Laguna where I had been given permission to park, when suddenly an elegantly trousered Mme. Dupont stepped into the beam of my headlights. They, too, had found April too hot on the south coast, and were spending their last weeks on this cool plateau, only twenty minutes' drive from Santa Cruz, 2,000 feet below, or from the mighty pine forest of La Esperanza, 2,000 feet above.

It was in another pine forest, above El Paso in the green well-watered island of La Palma, that I came across Kristina Lafquist, whom I had last encountered collecting mail at Cook's office in Santa Cruz de Tenerife. She was seated before a canvas which held a distant view of perhaps the most famous of all Canary pines, the Pino de la Virgen, beside the sanctuary from which it takes its name.

But it was beneath palms rather than pines—date palms bearing real dates—in the far west of Gomera, in the other-worldly valley of the Great King, that I found Mme. Neuve at the single café beside the beach. There we talked of all the friends we had made on another terrace, that of the *Parador* at Lanzarote, when we were both staying there, and in particular of a young German who sometimes drove into Arrecife from the lonely strand where he was camping down near Playa Blanca.

It is not only in Lanzarote, however, and not only in Fuerteventura, that I have met Franz Glück—for it was he. At Maspalomas in Gran Canaria and at San Marcos in Tenerife I have seen his little orange tent pitched. I have met him swimming at Arinaga and at Sardina, and sun-bathing at Las Cañadas. He even turned up in Hierro, smallest and remotest of the islands, on the very boat which a few hours later was to take me away. He knows the Canaries even better than I do, for he has achieved something which I shall never attempt: he has climbed all 12,152 feet of Mount Teide.

Going South

These visitors—they are more than mere tourists—who elect to spend month after month in the Canary sunshine, give life there a certain special flavour. But the main substance of that life is of course provided by the inhabitants, the *canarios* themselves. We shall be meeting them all the way through this book, so I shall say no more about them now. But there are certain other visitors to the islands whom we shall not meet, but to whom we ought to be introduced. Like ourselves, they came south. Liking what they found they stayed on, or, if they returned whence they came, carried back memories of western isles of the blest, temperate gardens of the Hesperides, which were to weave themselves into the myths of poets, the surmises of historians, and even the parables of philosophers.

Myths, surmises and parables are the stuff of mystery. And mystery surrounds not only these earlier visitors, but even the origin of the islands themselves. They are of volcanic rock throughout, and their subterranean fires are only quiescent. There was an eruption as recently as 1949 on La Palma. Brushwood thrown into a hole in the Fire Mountains of Lanzarote will burst into flame. It might be supposed, then, that the islands rose violently from the ocean bed, especially as profound trenches surround them and separate them from one another, trenches dropping sometimes as many feet below sea level as the islands' peaks tower above it.

The pre-scientific age, on the other hand, following willingly the philosopher's legend,[1] saw in the Canaries the last vestiges of a sunken continent, Plato's Atlantis. And even today the biologist, driven by the facts, demands what the geologist, supported in his turn by the facts, is unable to grant him. For the biologist finds there animals, birds and plants which can only have come from other lands, and in particular from southern Europe, and which must have required a bridge of land by which to cross.

Why could they not have been brought by men? Because they came south when no men existed to bring them.

Men have indeed brought much to the islands, including most of the animals and plants you will meet near the coasts and in other

[1] Plato, *Timaeus* and *Critias*.

accessible or cultivable areas. Goats, camels and donkeys, today Canary symbols, were all introduced, along with all the other domestic animals. So were the potato and the tomato, that recent enricher of the dry southlands of Gran Canaria and Tenerife. So was the banana, which now covers every *fanegada*[1] which can be flattened and irrigated. So was even the fig, although it is so rooted in Canary life and custom that on Hierro one can own a fig tree independently of the land on which it grows. The very prickly pear, without which it is hard to imagine a Canary landscape, was originally planted as a host for the cochineal insect.

But as one penetrates into higher and further regions these imported species are less in evidence. The characteristic forms of life are native, perfectly adapted over long ages to a harder environment, to which the intruders of a few centuries ago have not had the time to accustom themselves.

Thus the only four footed creatures to be found on the wavelashed rocks of Anaga north of Tenerife or of Salmor north of Hierro are great lizards up to two feet in length, the nearest surviving relations outside the New World and the far East of the giant reptiles of a hundred million years ago. In each island, too, exist birds which can only fly short distances, but which are closely similar to birds elsewhere, especially in Europe. They came south sufficiently long ago to have developed into distinct species; and sometimes different species of the same genus are even to be found on different islands.

It is above all the vegetation of the more inaccessible regions which is most genuinely Canary. Sometimes we can recognize its forms as cousins of species we know at home. The *Pinus canariensis* can only be a pine, although its bushier leaves yet somehow sparer construction would make it out of place in those glens of which the Scots pine is monarch; and although its greater size and intangibly Atlantic quality would disqualify it for Provençal hillside, Italian shore, or other habitat of the Mediterranean pine. The heaths up in the mountains of Gomera are of the same race as the humble heather of our own moorlands; but by some quirk of

[1] The Canary unit of square measure, which varies quite widely from island to island.

climate which Alice in Wonderland perhaps could explain, they have grown to such an extent that it is they who overlook us, sometimes from as much as twenty or thirty feet. And as you approach the summit of Mount Teide do not fear that the altitude has given you hallucinations if you see a tiny purple flower clinging to the rock. It is what it looks, a violet, but of a distinct species, *Viola cheiranthifolia*, which has so adapted itself to the height, the absence of soil, and the intense sunlight that with one small bird, *Fringilla teydea*, the Teide chaffinch, it is the only living thing to be found at over 10,000 feet.

All these forms of life must at some time have reached the islands somehow. Probably, like ourselves, they came south. For their nearest relations are more often found in Europe than in the adjoining parts of Africa.

But there are other native plants and trees, which bear no resemblance whatsoever to our own flora. They remind us, rather, of some fantasy world, or of a distorted vision of the jungles through which dinosaurs roamed and pterodactyls flew. There is the curious candelabra-shaped cactus-like *cardón*, or *Euphorbia canariensis*. There are untold acres of *retama* bushes over the eerie plains of Las Cañadas, whose white flowering each spring seems at first like another fall of snow, and brings a brief domestic murmur of bees to those lunar wastes 7,000 feet above the sea. There is above all the dragon tree, whose clumped and spiky leaves, blood-red sap and longevity have always inspired awe. Once this was awe of the magical, and we feel it no less because today it is inspired by scientific knowledge. For the dragon tree has been described as a living survivor of the forests of the tertiary era.

It is to those forests that we must look for the near relations of *Dracaena draco* and of many other plants found only in the Canaries. We shall find there no fossilised remains of those forests. For whether or not the islands existed in the tertiary age, volcanic rock by its nature holds no fossils. But if we turn to the fossilised forests of southern Europe of the period before the Ice Age we shall at once be struck by their resemblance to the Canary plant life of today. And we shall hazard the guess that these strange forms came south, to find in the islands a last refuge when the encroaching ice destroyed the far more extensive flora of which they once formed part.

The theory is neat and attractive. The botanist himself assures us that something like that must have happened. But the plants required a land connection to cross to the islands, and the geologist denies that such a connection has ever existed. He even tells us that at the beginning of the Ice Age the volcanoes of the islands were probably in active eruption—hardly conducive to colonisation by life of any kind.

This account of the first five days of creation in the Canaries has left unanswered as many problems as it has raised. It is as if the first chapter of Genesis had been written without the third verse, and we pray in vain 'Let there be light'. And the mysteries merely deepen as the sixth day opens.

For at last man, too, came south. He found, as we shall find, seven large islands which then had more trees, and therefore more water. He settled in all seven of them. And our next mystery is that when they emerge into the half-light of medieval history their inhabitants have no knowledge of navigation. It is as if they lived on six planets round the sun of Mount Teide, dimly descrying some of their neighbouring worlds, and all worshipping the same white cone above the clouds, but ignorant of whether those other planets were peopled by beings like themselves.

I speak of the half-light of medieval history. For it was only during the fourteenth and fifteenth centuries that the islands were by degrees incorporated into the outside world. Prehistoric in the Canary Islands means anything over five hundred years old.

The British islands, too, emerged from prehistory, when fifteen hundred years earlier they moved from dark night to bright sunshine with all the suddenness of a tropical dawn, in 55 B.C. But there were no Julius Caesars around, swiftly conquering and lucidly writing up their conquests, in the less confident, more fragmented world of Chaucer and Villon. To understand something of the difficulties of interpreting the early history of the Canaries it is worth pondering how little we know of what went on at the same period in Lancastrian and Yorkist England. If we know so little of our own land, then how much less likely are we to possess full accounts of newly discovered islands on the edge of the known world. Their discoverers and conquerors were in any case mainly preoccupied with Moors, with rival Portuguese or Aragonese, and soon with far greater discoveries and conquests across the Atlantic.

These circumstances under which the islands were discovered and occupied by Europeans mean that we may never know the answers to many questions about their earlier inhabitants. For the questions were never asked. The natives were not objects of anthropological research. They were enemies to be defeated. They were slaves to be sold. They were pagans to be baptized. Within half a century of conquest, moreover, the fusion between conquerors and conquered was all but complete. For the natives were also wives to wed.

Traditionally the Spaniards take their women where they find them, while the English, we are always told, import their own home-made product. The Spaniards may well have learnt this habit in the Canaries, which was their first conquest outside Europe, and where they first developed in miniature so many practices later applied in the New World.

They willingly took wives in the Canaries because the women there were eminently nubile. Even before conquest was assured conquistadores were conducting love affairs with beautiful native princesses such as Fayna in Lanzarote, Dácil in Tenerife, or Iballa in Gomera. Their beauty, to be recognized, had to conform to the canons of the society from which the newcomers came. The natives, in other words, were a white race. Had they not been, fusion would never have been so swift or so complete. For despite more than four centuries of intermarriage the populations of Latin America today separate like a three-tiered sandwich into white élite, half-bred *mestizos*, and Indians.

The blood of the earlier inhabitants still mingles, therefore, with that of the conquerors in the present population. 'There is not a family established fifty years in the islands,' declared a lecturer at La Laguna University before a packed auditorium in which I was perhaps the only non-Canary, 'in whose veins does not course *la fuerte sangre indigena*.' I could almost hear the strong native blood rising in pride all around me. But one tries in vain to distinguish which features come from which race, or in what proportion the two have come together in any one individual.

Their many skeletons and mummies tell us that the natives were big, well-made people; and their surviving scalps of apparently reddish-brown hair are some evidence for the tradition that they were fair-haired. In Tenerife a tall man with these characteristics and with large though not insensitive hands will be pointed out as a typical Guanche (the Guanches were the natives of Tenerife, although the name is frequently, and quite incorrectly, given to the pre-conquest inhabitants of all the islands).

Surveys of the present population also indicate that substantial numbers—about a third in most of the islands, but as many as 46 per cent in Gomera—are of the same Cro-Magnon type to which many of the mummies belong. The seat of the Cro-Magnon culture is indicated by its name, that of a village in south-west France. It was a branch of this intelligent, large-brained Cro-Magnon race, the Iberians, who gave their name to the peninsula shared by Spain and Portugal. This helps to explain the easy assimilation between the *canarios* and their conquerors. And if, as other evidence suggests, there was a certain admixture of semitic blood in the eastern islands, had there not also been an admixture of semitic blood in Spain itself, during the eight centuries of Moslem rule?

We are driven to measuring skulls and to comparing heights not only because historical sources are deficient at the moment when the islands at last enter history, but also because through no fault of her own the handmaiden of history, archaeology, can here do less than usual to help us. Islands which have only been created in geologically recent times and which are short of rain and of soil are unable to furnish us with those discoveries in depth which provide us with at least a broad account of the past of more ancient lands. The remains of man, whether early or late, are contained in a single shallow layer.

Even these never lend themselves to those fruitful parallels which have solved so many problems elsewhere. Here no stray coins indicate commercial contacts with more highly developed centres. In Europe and elsewhere styles of flint chipping or of pottery decoration can be claimed as evidence for association with other cultures, and thus a rough chronology can be built up. But the trained archaeologist arriving in the Canaries must be prepared to forget all his experience, and to examine what he sees without preconceptions.

'I know that the English don't mind jokes,' said Diego Cuscoy, director of the Archaeological Museum in Santa Cruz de Tenerife. 'And so I decided to play one on O. G. S. Crawford, the eminent British archaeologist who was on a visit here.'

Showing him a terracotta pot Cuscoy asked him: 'From your experience of Mediterranean and middle Eastern prehistory, what would you give as the date of this vessel?'

It did not take the distinguished visitor long to make up his mind. '1800 to 1500 B.C.,' he pronounced.

'Now will you put your hand inside the *vasija*,' said Cuscoy.

Crawford did so and drew out four nails.

'I found them inside, just as you have done, when I first discovered the vessel,' continued Cuscoy. 'Until the arrival of Europeans iron was unknown in the islands. Those nails are identical with those we know to have been used for shipbuilding in the fourteenth century A.D. So the *vasija* dates from about three thousand years later than you have suggested.'

The story also illustrates how the Canaries moved in one leap from the New Stone Age to the Iron Age. Not one trace of bronze, elsewhere the first metal worked by primitive man, has here been discovered. The conquistadores found themselves in contact with an untouched Neolithic culture, less advanced technically than that of the builders of Stonehenge.

But if the islands knew no Bronze Age, they knew no Old Stone Age either. If their inhabitants belonged to the Neolithic world only five hundred years ago, they belonged to it already when first they landed.

When did this first arrival take place? Despite the absence of all the usual archaeological clues, two ingenious methods have been used in an attempt to solve this problem. Unfortunately, however, they give two different answers.

The Atlantic launches an average of 350 waves an hour against the Canary coasts, and we can calculate the rate at which they are slowly being worn away. Applying this rate to certain caves which were once human habitations, but which are now largely eroded, or isolated by the sea, seems to indicate that men have been in the islands since 2000 or 2500 B.C.

The Carbon 14 technique, based on loss of radioactivity in certain substances, provides a more precise tool. It has been applied to a wide selection of mummies in Gran Canaria, and has come up with a series of dates ranging from A.D. 292 to A.D. 1082. This seems to differ by over two thousand years from the date given by the other method.

For even the first arrivals almost certainly embalmed their dead. Only in Fuerteventura have no mummies yet been found; and Fuerteventura is a large dry island whose small Neolithic population would leave less remains, which its small modern population would be less likely to discover. Embalmment is not a very widespread practice, and many writers have suggested that it reached the Canaries directly or indirectly from ancient Egypt.

Certainly after one look at an atlas the only reasonable answer to the question of where these first inhabitants came from would seem to be North Africa. And what little we know of their speech suggests affinities with Berber. Or so, at least, the experts tell us. There are not very many Berber experts about, and buried in the learned reviews of Las Palmas and of La Laguna lie high-flown studies of this fascinating subject, written with the imagination and the academic venom which only a remote cul-de-sac of uncharted prehistory can evoke. Even the layman shudders at the trigger-happy use of such epithets as 'neo-punic' in connection with isolated carvings on distant Hierro.

However, the surviving vocabularies of the various islands do sometimes appear to coincide; and all share the same family look, at least as much as do the different Celtic or Latin languages. The Austrian D. J. Wölfel, who had given as much time to this study as anyone, wrote not long before his death in the *Revista de Historia de Canarias* of 1958:

'. . . all authors who really understood one of the island languages confirm the reciprocal understanding between the islands, despite material differences. An aboriginal of Gran Canaria, of about 1530, declared the three languages of Gran Canaria, Tenerife, and Gomera to be related, and all three to be similar to that of the *zenagas* of the African coast. The linguistic material of all the islands which has reached us shows in every part the same formation of the words and precisely an authentically Berber formation.'

Knowing how few and how late are our sources on those early years when the native languages still survived, I would dearly love to know who were 'all the authors who really understood' one of them. However even the sceptical Señor Cuscoy is prepared to accept, with reservations, the argument in favour of a relationship between them and Berber, or rather, the relationship of both to a common ancestor. But he will topple the imaginative enquirer from any too eagerly reached conclusions with a delightfully quizzical 'Do you speak Berber?'

This relationship not only seems natural, but goes some way towards explaining the mysteries associated with the early inhabitants of the Canaries. For the Berbers are themselves a mysterious race, whose very existence is even now hardly recognized by the average educated man.

Found to this day in several countries of North Africa, they have been without a land of their own for longer than the people of Israel. But they are far from unknown to history, although their wars of self-determination never bore that title. They resisted the Carthaginian colonization of their coastline. Later, united in the kingdom of Numidia, they co-operated with the Romans in the defeat and destruction of the great Phoenician city, only to be themselves included soon afterwards in the *pax romana*.

Included but not absorbed. It has been shown (by H. W. Friend in *The Donatist Church*) that the Donatist heresy which divided the North African Christians from the fourth to the seventh centuries was a reflection in ecclesiastical terms of the Berbers' discontent against the Roman ruling class. These same Berbers were a thorn in the side of Vandals and Byzantines, and to them must go the credit for the fifty year hiatus in the Moslem conquest of North Africa. When at the end of the seventh century the Berber tribes themselves became Moslems the advance regained momentum, and within a few years had swept beyond the Straits of Gibraltar and over the Pyrenees.

Allies of the Arabs from then onwards, they remained nevertheless a separate race, which even in this century has attracted the world's attention in the Rif wars of the 1920s, and in the revolt of the Berbers of Kabylia against the newly independent Algeria which their courage had helped to found. For they are not Semitic, although their language has inevitably over the centuries collected a large Semitic vocabulary. By no means all the fair-haired children running around the Berber villages are a memorial to Vikings, to Crusaders, or to Christian additions to their harems brought back by the Barbary pirates.

More skull measuring, with blood sampling to show the proportion of rhesus negative individuals, has led some anthropologists to hazard a relationship between the Berbers and that other mysterious race, the Basques. And if the Basques, as seems probable, are the last survivors of the Cro-Magnon, 'Iberian', pre-Aryan population of Western Europe, one is tempted to guess that the Berbers are the survivors of the same Cro-Magnon, 'Iberian', pre-Semitic population of North Africa, of whom the aboriginal *canarios* were the far western extension.

We must return to the mystery of how these 'proto-Berbers'—as we ought to call them if we accept the above argument—reached islands if when discovered by Europeans they knew nothing of navigation. One suggestion is that they were brought there by other seafaring races, who did not settle there themselves.

But this seems almost as far-fetched as Thor Heyerdahl's elaboration of his *Kon-tiki* hypothesis. According to this the Peruvians not only crossed the Pacific to Polynesia, but had earlier crossed the Atlantic from Egypt, passing by the Canaries and leaving the practice of embalmment as a souvenir of their stay. This has received the witty comment: '. . . these hypotheses have come to animate our studies, and in the sporting era in which we live they can serve as pretext for magnificent expeditions'.[1]

[1] L. Pericot, *Anuario de Estudios Atlanticos*, Volume I, 1955. This particular hypothesis has indeed served as pretext to another of Thor Heyerdahl's 'magnificent expeditions' since these words were written.

Going South

Of the many arguments that I have read by writers dearly anxious to prove prehistoric Atlantic crossings I cannot help repeating the one which appears the subtlest and most convincing, although it has no direct connection with the Canaries. Wild cotton, it seems, has two varieties: an American with thirteen small chromosomes, and an Old World with thirteen large chromosomes. But the cells of the variety of domestic cotton already cultivated in Peru before the time of Christ have twenty-six chromosomes, thirteen large, and thirteen small; and this domestic cotton must therefore have been a hybrid of the two wild varieties.

Another suggestion is that the Moslem invasions of the seventh century were responsible for ending maritime contact between the aboriginals and the Berbers from whom they had sprung. But this runs counter to an argument that it was the drying of the Sahara and the Moslem invasion which led to the peopling of the Canaries in the first place—an argument which would tally with the Carbon 14 results.

My own view, for what it is worth, is that the first inhabitants arrived in their own boats, and then over the years simply forgot how to use them. Once in the Hesperides, where the sun always shines and the golden apples are forever ripe, why move on? As Roy Plomley asks each castaway at the end of Desert Island Discs: 'Would you try to escape?' The proto-Berbers answered 'No.'

They were not the last visitors who elected to stay put in Paradise, as anyone will testify who has run across today's colonies of brandy-soaked expatriates in the Canaries. And in a strange way the mild climate and the lack of stimulus acted on the noble savages just as on the seedy sophisticates. Both degenerated.

The very fact that the aboriginals seem to have forgotten the art of building and using the boats which brought them is a serious example of their 'having lost qualities proper to their race, sunk from their former excellence', as the dictionary defines 'degenerate'. And the consequent isolation from each other on their seven islands meant that they developed seven separate cultures, just as over the ages on each of the Galapagos Islands there has developed a slightly different species of giant tortoise.

These seven cultures had much in common. We have already

noted that they shared ignorance of metals, a common ancestor of their closely related languages, and the custom of embalming their dead. But these cultures were more differentiated from each other than the Galapagos tortoises. In particular, archaeologists early remarked a strong contrast between those of the two most important islands, Gran Canaria and Tenerife.

The *canarios*, or natives of Gran Canaria (the term is also used of the present day inhabitants of the whole archipelago), had made several technical advances over the Guanches. Often they lived in stone huts rather than in caves. They wore clothes woven from dried rushes rather than the skins of animals. Above all their pottery is of more complex design and more sophisticated workmanship, the clay often being mixed with stone dust to prevent cracking. It includes small terracotta idols and seal-like objects called *pintaderas* found in none of the other islands.

Archaeology shows that the ancestors of these *canarios* of the fifteenth century led a relatively simpler life; a similar life, in fact, to that of the ancestors of the fifteenth-century Guanches. But the Guanches of the time of the conquest led a simpler life still. They had forgotten not only navigation, but also how to decorate their pitchers and platters. Whereas the culture of Gran Canaria was progressive, therefore, that of Tenerife was regressive. In the strictly dictionary sense the Guanches had degenerated.

This puzzling divergence has received a simple and intellectually satisfying explanation. It seems probable that Gran Canaria, and to a lesser extent all the other islands except Tenerife and perhaps Gomera, received more than one wave of settlers, and possibly other visitors too. These later arrivals brought at once new techniques and stimulus to a stagnant society. And some of them may have brought some form of writing.

Explanations of the mysterious inscriptions found on several of the islands must share the prize in the contest in academic lunacy which has tempted so many investigators of Canary prehistory. Many a would-be Michael Ventris has sought a key to the writings of the Hesperideans such as he found to the writings of the Minoans.

But they have a harder code to crack than Linear B. It is in fact

1. Lanzarote: setting off to climb the Fire Mountains (p. 57)

2. Lanzarote: volcanic ash spread over the fields both attracts dew and prevents evaporation (p. 54)

3. Lanzarote at its most lunar, with vines, each in its miniature 'crater', set against a background of dead volcanoes (pp. 53-5)

4. Lanzarote: herdsman at Macher, near La Tiñosa

5. Lanzarote: preparing the ash for planting-out of the tomato seedlings (p. 54)

6. Lanzarote: the largest fishing fleet in the Canaries is based at Arrecife (p. 48)

Going South

For it has already been emphasized that the word degenerate can only be used of the Guanches in a purely technical sense. They were a fine race living in an earthly paradise, who in simplifying their way of life over the centuries were perhaps refining it. When in the high tide of the Enlightenment the islands brought forth a great historian to tell their story—an Archdeacon of Fuerteventura, born in Tenerife, who died in Las Palmas—he saw in their early inhabitants the noble savage so admired by contemporary writers in France:

'All their contracts and sales consisted, as in the time of the Trojan War, in exchange and barter. Barley against sheep: cheeses against honey: figs against skins. Their conversation was neither of gold nor of silver, nor of jewels, nor of the rest of the usual goods dependent on fancy or on faulty judgement. It was rather of rains in due season, of fruitful sowings, of rich pastures, of happy breedings. Quiet sleep, sweet peace, the fertility of their wives, the strength of their arms, the blessing of heaven poured over their cattle and flocks, granaries and barns: all these were necessary possessions, simple and innocent, which our vanity cannot lessen in value.'

Figs, although already an important part of their 'necessary possessions' at the time of the conquest, had only been introduced about a century earlier. Sheep, too, had probably only been available for a few years to barter against barley. The bones of goats are constantly found in association with aboriginal remains, and goat-skins were always used for wrapping the mummies. But no trace of sheep has been discovered on any prehistoric sites. Figs and sheep were then perhaps the last innocent gifts of the outside world to islanders whose way of life was soon to be as violently shattered as that of the nineteenth-century Tahitians.

The outside world, however, moved in at a slower pace to embrace the North Atlantic than it moved in to embrace the South Pacific. Twice, as the light of a civilization grew more powerful, the Canaries appeared briefly and blurred in its penumbra, only to be lost again in the night of ignorance.

That the first of these civilizations, the Graeco-Roman, should have become aware of the Canaries is hardly surprising. It is more surprising that it did not learn more about them, and indeed absorb them. Rome subdued the deserts of northern Arabia, the dense forests of central Europe, and the bleak hills of southern Scotland. Why did she not add to her empire the mild Hesperides, standing little further towards the limits of the known world than these less welcoming regions?

Perhaps because there was no external stimulus: threatening Parthians, Dacians, or Caledonians, clamouring for her presence there. It is significant that the two leading figures of the Roman world whom we know to have taken an interest in the Canaries ruled not in Rome itself, but instead in the two regions with which the islands' subsequent history was to be linked.

Anyone with right-wing sympathies might describe Quintus Sertorius as the Ian Smith of the Roman world. In exile in Spain he founded there a new Rome, closer in spirit to the ideals of the Roman republic which sent its armies against him. This experiment lasted barely ten years. But it remains one of the most intriguing might-have-beens of history how long it might have continued, and with what results, if he had transferred it to an even remoter theatre. For in flight from his enemies about the year 82 B.C. his fleet touched land somewhere near Huelva, where, so Plutarch[1] tells us:

'He found there some mariners lately arrived from the Atlantic islands. These are two in number, separated from each other by a narrow channel, and lying at the distance of ten thousand furlongs from the African coast. They are called "The Fortunate Islands". Rain seldom falls there, and then falls moderately; while they have usually soft breezes, which scatter such rich dews, that the soil is not only good for sowing and planting, but spontaneously produces the most excellent fruits; and those in such abundance, that the inhabitants have only to indulge themselves in the enjoyment of ease and leisure. The air is always pleasant and salubrious, through the happy temperature of the seasons, and their insensible transition into each other. For the north and the east winds, which

[1] Plutarch, *Life of Sertorius*.

blow from our continent, are dissipated and lost in the immense interval; and the sea winds (that is, the south and the west) bring with them from the ocean slight and gentle showers, but still more frequently only a refreshing moisture, which imperceptibly scatters plenty over their plains. Hence it is generally believed, even among the barbarians, that these are the Elysian Fields and the seats of the blessed, which Homer has described in all the charms of verse.'

It would be impossible to find better words in which to paint the Canaries' climate, right down to the 'rich dews' and the 're-freshing moisture' on which, as we shall see, agriculture in certain places still depends. The noble Roman was almost seduced.

'Sertorius, hearing these wonders, conceived a strong desire to settle in those islands, where he might live in perfect tranquillity, at a distance from the evils of tyranny and war'.

The evils of tyranny and war, however, dragged him back to-wards the Mediterranean, and it was Augustus's satellite-king, Juba II of Mauretania (Morocco), who actually sent an expedition to explore the Fortunate Islands perhaps three quarters of a century later (he reigned from 25 B.C. to about A.D. 23). The works of this learned prince—they included a treatise on the cactus-like *euphorbia*, named after his physician Euphorbus—have been lost, but Pliny the Elder[1] repeats some of what he wrote about the islands, of which by that time six are known.

Five are named: Ombrios, Junonia with 'a small temple . . . built of only a single stone', Capraria 'which swarms with large lizards; and, in view from these islands, Ninguario, so named from its perpetual snow, and wrapped in cloud; and next to it one named Canaria, from its multitude of dogs of a huge size (two of these were brought back for Juba). Juba said that in this island there were traces of buildings; that while they all had an abundant supply of fruit and of birds of every kind, Canaria also abounded in palm-groves bearing dates, and in conifers. . . .'

Thus for the first time the name Canaria appears in history.

---

[1] Pliny, *Natural History*, Book VI, xxxvii.

Argument still rages as to which individual islands these descriptions refer to, though none quarrel with the identification of Ninguario as Tenerife. Other doubts concern the 'Purple Islands' (where purple dye-stuffs were found) from which the *Fortunatae* lay at 625 miles' sail to the south-west, and whether the mention of only six islands can be explained by a land-bridge linking Lanzarote to Fuerteventura 2,000 years ago. (My own view is that anyone passing them at some distance would regard them as one island even today.)

That so much should have been learnt about them, and with such accuracy, was due to the accidental presence of an enterprising and highly cultured ruler in the nearest part of the civilized world. When, after the death of Juba's son in A.D. 40, Mauretania became two more Roman provinces like any others, there disappeared the resources and the stimulus which might have mounted other expeditions.

The northern Mauretanian province, Tingitana (from Tingis, the modern Tangiers)—it almost exactly corresponded to the twentieth-century Spanish protectorate in northern Morocco—was attached by the Emperor Diocletian to Spain, and thus passed, at least in theory, under the rule of the Visigoths in the fifth century. Amongst the competing Christian kingdoms of medieval Spain, Castile always claimed to be the sole rightful heir of the Visigothic monarchy; and her acceptance of overlordship of the Canaries, and her interest in them, years before they became useful as a stage on the route to the Indies, were therefore partly due to their association with Juba.

Their next recorded visitors, however, came from amongst the real, rather than the merely titular occupiers of the land he had once ruled. These were the Arabs, who rediscovered them about 1016, and named them Kaledat. But, like the Romans, they did no more than vaguely recognize the fact of their existence. With the fourteenth century, however, began a more permanent relationship with the outside world.

The first meetings were accidental. In 1291 a member of the great Doria family of Genoa sent two galleys under the command of the brothers Vadino and Ugolino Vivaldi with a view to following the route taken by the Carthaginian Hanno nearly 2,000 years earlier, and perhaps achieving the circumnavigation of Africa. Like him, they may have touched briefly at the Canaries, but we shall never know, for they were never heard of again. Expeditions searching for them some years later certainly did visit the islands: thus we hear of Lancellotto (or Lanzaroto) Malocello who built a tower on Lanzarote, the island which still bears his name.

This may have been in 1312; but the mysteries surrounding the European occupation of the Canaries are only relatively less than those which obscure the details of their prehistoric settlement. What little we know we know largely by chance.

In 1827, for example, there came to light in a library in Florence a fragment of a diary kept by the great writer Boccaccio. In the course of this diary he transcribed a letter from certain Florentine merchants living in Seville, who describe an expedition—otherwise unknown—fitted out in 1341 by Alfonso IV of Portugal, the kingdom which was to take a more direct interest in the islands than Castile over the next 125 years.

This expedition, consisting of three boats under yet another Genoese, Angiolino di Tegghia, found thirteen islands, only five of which appeared inhabited. They noted that Gran Canaria, then as now, was better cultivated in the north than in the south. They described Tenerife's mountain of almost 30,000 paces high, topped by 'a white body like a castle or sharp rock, with on its peak a furnace light which rose and fell alternately.' More surprisingly, they found either Fuerteventura or Lanzarote (it is impossible to say which from the description) not only 'abundant in goats', but 'covered in trees'.

Two years earlier the Majorcan cartographer Angelino Dolcet had included these last two islands in his projection of the world. The Canaries were at last on the map.

They were soon to enter political calculations, though at first chimerically enough, in the unfulfilled dreams of the hollow-crowned Prince of Fortune, Luis de la Cerda. For the moment those who actually reached the islands sought something more immediately profitable than an empty dominion. They sought slaves, then a highly marketable commodity in all the lands bordering the Mediterranean.[1] For slavery was in the fourteenth century a recognized institution throughout western Europe. Even in England it was only after the labour shortage caused by the Black Death of 1346 that the 'bond man' gradually began to disappear from the manorial rolls.

And so we hear of expeditions—in reality raiding parties—of Majorcans, Aragonese, Viscayans, which descended with increasing frequency on the Canaries during the second half of the century. Those of which record has reached us are no doubt but a small proportion of the total. But although some of these visitors stayed on the islands for shorter or longer periods, and some even made attempts at evangelization, none of them arrived with the considered aim of conquest and settlement.

Until, on 1st May 1402, Jean de Béthencourt, Sieur de Sigy in Normandy, set sail from La Rochelle to go south.

[1] Recent research by Doctora Vicenta Cortés on the records of Valencia slave market makes a grim commentary on a rather later period of Canary history. Canary slaves begin to appear in the records for 1489 (after the suppression of the rebellion in Gomera), rise rapidly to a maximum during the years from 1493 to 1496 (when La Palma and Tenerife were being conquered), and disappear after 1502, when pacification was complete. The records contain fascinating lists of native names, although many had been baptised, generally taking names of members of the royal family such as Juan, Isabel and Catalina.

Women on average fetched about 25 per cent more than men, although far more women than men were offered for sale. Doctora Cortés suggests as the reason for this that the men were generally slaughtered, and their wives and children preserved for enslavement. This is begging the question: we simply do not know what proportion of the natives were killed off during or after the conquest.

The American historians Cook, Borah, and Simpson have in recent years been able to show that the population of Mexico, some twenty-five million when Hernán Cortés landed, had sunk to about a quarter of that figure by 1547. It is a pity that their methods of research, based on the very full tribute returns available, cannot be applied to the Canaries. For they would illuminate not only the conquest of the islands, but the whole story of Spain's expansion overseas, of which this formed the opening chapter.

❧ 2 ❧

Lanzarote

How had someone from distant Normandy heard about the Canaries in 1402? Because their first great export had been distributed over a far wider market than we might expect. For Béthencourt was able to take with him as interpreters two Canary natives —they had been christened Isabel and Alfonso—whom he had acquired in Normandy.

He took also two chaplains, Pierre Boutier and Jean le Verrier, and it is their account of his expedition, or perhaps a later account based on their diaries, which forms the first continuous document of Canary history. It is worth repeating here the first few lines of *Le Canarien*, as their story is called, for its style and old French perfectly convey the atmosphere of that world of Froissart and Malory of which Béthencourt himself was so typical.

'Ung temps jadis souloit on mettre en escript les bonnes chevalleries et les estranges choses que les vaillans conquereurs souloient faire au temps passé, ainssi que on trouve en enciennes ystoires. Voulons nous yci faire mencion de l'emprinse que Bethencourt, chevalier et baron nez du royaulme de France en Normandie, lequel Bethencourt se parti de son hostel de Granville la Tainturiere en Caulx et s'en vint à La Rochelle; et la trouva Gadiffer de La Salle, ung bon et honneste chevalier, lequel aloit a son adventure. Et out parolles entre le dit Bethencourt et Gadiffer et lui demanda Monseigneur de Bethencourt quel part il vouloit tirer, et le dit Gadiffer disoit qu'il aloit à son adventure. Adonc Mons. de Bethencourt lui dit qu'il estoit fort joieulx de l'avoir trouvé et lui demanda se il lui plaisoit de venir en sa compagnie, en contant au dit Gadiffer son entreprinse, et tant que le dit Gadiffer fut tout joieulx de l'ouir parler et de l'emprinse qui estoit faicte par le dit Bethencourt'.[1]

Don Quixote himself could not have summed up the wandering knight's chivalrous motivation more succinctly than Gadifer de la Salle: *'il aloit a son adventure.'* This was the very period when Béthencourt's enemies, the English, used to organize those 'free companies' which ranged from the Atlantic to the Adriatic, selling their services and seeking adventure. And this was very much what Béthencourt was doing. As the plain-spoken Victorian Mrs. Olivia Stone put it, he 'got up an expedition to the islands.'

I am insisting on Béthencourt's period because only with his period in mind can we appreciate this tragi-comic meeting between Medieval and Neolithic man. It was a period when logistics were simple. After their initial establishment on Lanzarote Béthencourt returned to Europe for reinforcements, and sent off 'a frigate . . . equipped with eighty recruits, and loaded with four pipes of wine, sixteen sacks of flour, and other provisions of mouth and war.'

It was the period of feudalism, of protection given in return for homage rendered. Béthencourt acquired the funds for equipping the above frigate from the King of Castile, whom he in return acknowledged as overlord of his newly gained realm.

It was the period when Henry IV reigned in England, when a company of men-at-arms such as Béthencourt led south would include not only a knight like Gadifer de la Salle seeking adventure, but more than one Bardolph, and more than one ancient Pistol. And to whom are we to liken Bertin de Berneval, who led a wild mutiny during Béthencourt's absence in Castile, consuming the reserves of provisions, raping the women, and leaving Gadifer de la Salle unsuccoured on the dry islet of Lobos? To whom but to Falstaff himself?

These men, lifted almost literally from some battle of the Hundred Years War, seem out of place as they sail south from Cadiz

---

[1] There are in fact two versions of *Le Canarien*. This extract is taken from the one which plays down the part played by Gadifer de la Salle, probably being altered by a later Béthencourt. But as the alteration itself took place about 1490, it preserves the essential spirit of the age.

LANZAROTE

ALEGRANZA

Miles
0 — 5 — 10

Roque del Oeste
MONTAÑA CLARA
Las Conchas Beach
La Sociedad
GRACIOSA
Roque del Este
El Rio
La Batería
Orzola
Máguez
Haria
Cueva de los Verdes
Beach of Famara
La Caleta
La Santa
Cuesto de los Valles
Tinajo
Teguise
Tao
Mancha Blanca
Islote de Hilario
Timanfaya
San Bartolomé
El Golfo
La Gería
El Charco
Lake Janubio
Uga
Yaiza
Arrecife
San Gabriel Castle
Femes
La Tiñosa
RUBICON
Torre del Aguila
Playa Blanca
Punta de Papagayo

SPAIN
Gibraltar
Madeira
700 MILES

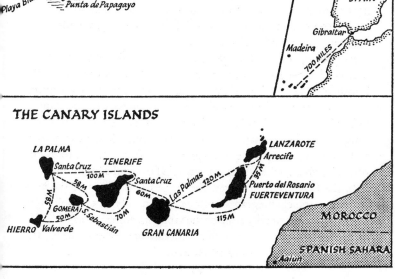

THE CANARY ISLANDS

LA PALMA
Santa Cruz
TENERIFE
LANZAROTE
Arrecife
100 M
Santa Cruz
120 M
37 M
98 M
58 M
60 M
Las Palmas
Puerto del Rosario
FUERTEVENTURA
GOMERA
S. Sebastián
70 M
HIERRO
Valverde
50 M
GRAN CANARIA
115 M
MOROCCO
SPANISH SAHARA
Aaiun

towards a land last known to literature in classical times. But we shall feel at least as strange ourselves as we approach Lanzarote, whether—as is more likely—we visit it from Las Palmas, or whether we travel on one of the ships for which it is the first port of call on leaving the Peninsula.

'La Peninsula': even to hear the phrase which the *canarios* always use to describe Spain is to feel oneself already going south. Those with the time to spare should always come by way of the Peninsula. Only thus can they hope to savour the special Canary flavour. Only thus, having just tasted Spain itself, can they be sure of finding something more than another group of Spanish islands. 'La Peninsula,' uttered on a soft, slow, dying note has the same power to evoke all the sweet melancholy of Canary speech as *'la guagua,'* or a distant strain of *'la farola del mar,'* deservedly the best known of all the island songs.

Lanzarote, however, seems sufficiently strange from whichever point of the compass we approach it. Going south in the winter we shall wake each dawn to a warmer world. Our overcoat is already cast aside at Cadiz. Next day comes the turn of our jacket. By the following evening we are in shirt-sleeves, and wondering whether the next morning we shall be sunbathing. But when the next morning comes, before even we have had time to find our shorts, comes that excited cry which in any language sounds much the same, and which spells landfall.

Alegranza, 'the joyful,' perhaps expresses this same thrill experienced by earlier travellers south at their first sight of the Fortunate Islands. (We must be careful, however, of accepting facile explanations of our islands' names: Lanzarote from Lancellotto Malocello is the only sure derivation.) It is only a small island, roughly circular in shape, and about two and a half miles across, and there may seem little to distinguish it from other bare rocky islets elsewhere, which bear but a single farm and a lighthouse.

In the first place, however, the jagged abruptness of the 700-feet hill in which Alegranza culminates can only be volcanic. It is an example on a smaller scale of the same phenomenon as El Golfo on Hierro: the phenomenon of a semi-circular crater of which the other half has slipped away into the sea.

Lanzarote

In the second place, the combination of brilliant light and of heavy ocean swell tells us that this island would find no place amongst Hebrides or Cyclades, the two groups of which we are reminded by the seascape opening before us.

For by now other islands have come into view. There is Montaña Clara, little more than a huge rock, and beside it Roque del Oeste, as its name implies a rock pure and simple. And away to the east we can descry the rather larger Roque del Este.

Beyond all these lies what seems by comparison a continent. There is a glimpse of golden sand, and then a whole range of dark, menacing peaks succeeding one another until they are lost to sight over the horizon.

Even those who have travelled widely may sense that these mountains are unlike any others they have seen. Yet they will certainly have seen many volcanoes before: extinct volcanoes in central France or even within Great Britain; still active volcanoes in Italy or Sicily or Japan. But never before will they have seen massed together some three hundred volcanoes of which a number were in eruption only two centuries ago.

The range is not in fact as long as it appears, the more distant hills belonging to Fuerteventura, which from here seems continuous with her northern neighbour. And the golden beach on the point of land nearest to us belongs to Graciosa, an island three times the size of Alegranza, which is separated from Lanzarote by a mile wide channel called El Rio ('the river').

It was in El Rio that Béthencourt first cast anchor, and Graciosa was the setting of a number of minor incidents during the early months of the conquest. But it has never since been anywhere near the centre of Canary life, and today, with its sand and its silence, it is the ultima Thule for a visitor to the archipelago. Landing from the launch which has brought him there directly from Arrecife, or by the shorter crossing from the fishing hamlet of Orzola, he will feel that the way of life which meets him—a few patches of vegetables for cultivation, a few camels for transport—is both simple and immemorial.

Yet not so many years ago this way of life was simpler still. The people of Graciosa lived from fish alone, and lived miserably. Until a far-sighted Captain-General of the Canaries named García, one of those fine proconsuls of whom the Spaniards can number as many as any imperial race, divided amongst the few households part of the land which until then had all been held in common. He further presented them with a couple of dozen camels with which to work it. His son still takes an interest in Graciosa, which reveres the father's memory. Well it may, for roots in the soil— both literally and metaphorically—and pride of ownership have brought modest prosperity. The population of the two villages, La Sociedad the 'capital,' and the smaller Pedro Barba has risen to over seven hundred, and the island now has the supreme status symbol amongst Canary villages: a cemetery.[1]

By hard work a man there can even rise to wealth. For in pesetas Don Jorge Toledo must now be a millionaire several times over. His fortune has been founded on the boats which link Graciosa with the outside world. He now owns several, each faster and more modern than the one before. He is, therefore, naturally aware of the advantages to be gained from attracting tourists. As *alcalde* or mayor he has promoted the sale of small building plots on which foreign purchasers are invited to erect suitably styled holiday homes from which to enjoy Graciosa's great golden beach of Las Conchas.

There was no thought of any foreigner buying plots on Graciosa when early in 1960 I saw the rather older boat which then linked it with the 'mainland' nosing its way past the *Parador* into the harbour of Arrecife. I returned the passengers' stare, for every one

[1] I have many times been told 'We have our own cemetery,' where in England the boast would have been of possessing a supermarket, a cinema, a post-office or a bank. This is because until recently there was generally only one cemetery for each administrative division. Some of these administrative divisions are not only large, but stretch across difficult country split up by deep chasms, *barrancos*: e.g. Garafía in the north of La Palma, or Tirajana in the south of Gran Canaria. A death amongst the poverty-stricken inhabitants of Maspalomas in the pre-tomato era meant not only mourning, but a gruelling trek with the body up the long Barranco de Fataga to San Bartolomé de Tirajana. (The name Tirajana gives the game away: the huge divisions are based on forgotten native tribal territories.)

of the women wore the traditional costume of Lanzarote: a uniformity in older ways which is now rare.

The description of this costume must wait, for our own ship is in its turn approaching Arrecife, the capital and port of Lanzarote. Since 1960 a new quay has been built two miles to the north-east, and we can no longer enjoy the pleasure, still allowed us at Fuerteventura, Gomera and La Palma, of stepping almost directly from our floating hotel into the life of the town.

There are other innovations: the coastline for five miles to the north-east of town, and for ten miles to the south-west, has been split up into building lots, on many of which houses have already risen. On my last visit a towering hotel was nearing completion near La Tiñosa. And on rising ground not far away an English-speaking school, run by some enterprising teachers from Jacksonville, Florida, opened in 1967. Most significant of all, there now stands near the new quay that dream of all small dry islands: a *potabilizadora,* or plant for the distillation of sea water.

That there are so few of these in a world which needs so many is due to their high capital cost. Lanzarote could never have installed one of its own. Here, as in other aspects of the island's development, it is mainly American capital which seems to be at work. On my last visit the state-owned hotel or *Parador* was packed with disappointed English tourists who had taken too literally a light-hearted article on Lanzarote in the *Sunday Express*. But I sensed that the solid buying of real estate came from across the Atlantic. The most active property agency in Arrecife even had a dynamic American blonde as partner.

The development of a retirement community for senior citizens, or of a family and leave base for oil and mining company staff working on concessions in nearby Spanish West Africa have been suggested as reasons for this American interest. The island is not big: no point is as far as twenty-five miles from the capital over roads which by Canary standards are straight and level. It might be thought that its distinctive way of life is doomed by the new invasion.

It is with the older Lanzarote that this chapter will concern itself. And there are two excellent reasons for supposing that the reader will find it still flourishing when he goes to see it for himself. For foreign expatriates and tourists, and in particular American expatriates and tourists, will tend to stay close to the yellow sands of the south-east coast. And Lanzarote's way of life has grown up in response to a special environment, an environment which still exists, and which has offered a greater challenge over the years than will be offered by a few hundred newcomers.

The nature of this challenge soon becomes apparent as we drive into Arrecife over land which seems not merely dry but dead. Not a blade is to be seen, and when after threading our way between the whitewashed houses of the main street we reach the public garden which lines the waterfront of the old harbour, we notice that in place of flowers and shrubs it is decorated with cunningly chosen blocks of strangely twisted lava.

The chances are that a wind will be blowing across this garden, for a wind of some sort blows in most places in Lanzarote for most of the time. So that when the sky is clouded over we shall be cool —though never cold. But even on cloudy days the light which is reflected across the old harbour from the eighteenth-century castle of San Gabriel has a clear, serene quality, empty of the menace which always attends a grey cloudy day in the north. And in Lanzarote we shall soon learn to live with clouds, some of which are never absent from the clearest sky. For these clouds practically never spell rain.

The castle of San Gabriel stands on part of a reef (in Spanish *arrecife*) which has given the town its name, and which gives shelter to the largest fishing fleet in the islands. The fleet brings back to the canning factory on the waterfront the rich harvest of the coasts of the Rio de Oro only sixty miles away. Perhaps because it is so much closer to its fishing grounds many of its craft in 1966 still boasted the noble lateen sail, which everywhere else has given way to the more prosaic motive power of diesel.

All the Canary capitals except Valverde on Hierro are the ports of their respective islands as well as the administrative centres. But in the other six islands someone in a distant village looking for a lift will enquire 'Are you going to the capital?' or 'Are you going to the city?' Only in Lanzarote will the question be 'Are you going to the *puerto?*' This must be because until two hundred years ago Arrecife was the port and nothing more. The capital was Teguise, seven miles inland, out of reach of hit-and-run raids by the Moors.

This accounts for the town's rather uninteresting appearance, and for the absence of any important monuments except for the castle already mentioned and another of the same period on the shore. The office of the Cabildo Insular,[1] the insular government, is almost indistinguishable from the houses and shops on either side of it in the main street. The church is a solid building, as well it might be, since it is built, like the rest of the town, from lava. But Arrecife would be a dull place if every wall had not been painted a bright white, with only a few corner-stones left in their natural state for contrast.

If one shuts one's eyes to the architecture, it is a far from boring place to stay in. It is neither a big city like Las Palmas or Santa Cruz de Tenerife, with almost too much noise and bustle, nor a backwater like Valverde or Puerto Rosario, where the silence of the empty streets can be unnerving. It belongs, rather, with Santa Cruz de la Palma and San Sebastián de la Gomera, to that middle rank of Canary capitals, where life is slow and sleepy, but where plenty is always happening on a small scale. It even has an advantage over these last two towns in being more intimately linked with the island of which it is the capital. For not only is Lanzarote lower; but its greatest altitudes are in the extreme north and east, as far as they could be from Arrecife, so that its communications with the country villages are over relatively level roads. The journey into town from an outlying part of Gomera or La Palma, both smaller islands than Lanzarote, can take four hours and cost

[1] Since 1927 the Canaries form two provinces, each with a civil governor like the forty-seven provinces of peninsular Spain. The province of Santa Cruz de Tenerife includes Tenerife, Gomera, La Palma, and Hierro. The province of Las Palmas de Gran Canaria includes Gran Canaria, Fuerteventura and Lanzarote. But geography dictates the retention of a certain autonomy by each island, dating from the time when a royal Captain-General presided over the whole archipelago, and for most purposes 'the government' as seen by *canarios* is that of their own island, the Cabildo, with its offices in the capital and its departments for roads, agriculture and so on.

as much as nine shillings one way, and merits careful consideration. But the inhabitant of Teguise, of Yaiza, or even of Haría in the far north thinks nothing of slipping down to the *puerto* for a mere morning's business.

These easy communications make the distinctive traditional dress which has survived amongst the countrywomen of Lanzarote an everyday sight in the town. It consists of a long dress, often black, with a white headscarf which comes not merely under but over the chin and round the cheeks. The wide-brimmed overhanging straw hat is the same as that worn everywhere by both sexes in the Canary villages—we may be wearing one ourselves before we sail home. But here it bears a deep black ribbon round the crown.

The curiously worn headscarf is generally explained as a protection against sun and wind. But the vaguely oriental look which it gives to its wearers reminds us how near we are to North Africa, from which so many raiding parties were launched against Lanzarote in the sixteenth and seventeenth centuries. Anthropologists, too, believe that a substantial proportion of Semitic blood mingles with that of Europeans and natives in the veins of the present inhabitants.

All the guide books will tell you that the best place to see this dress is amongst the vendors in the market held every morning in an open courtyard off the street leading from the church down towards the waterfront. Quite half the thirty or so stallholders will be in traditional dress; but we shall learn here that it conceals no mysteries. There is no oriental inscrutability about these women, whose homely crying of their wares proclaims them of the same earthy roots as their sisters in the markets of Málaga and Alicante. The oranges and bananas will have been imported into Lanzarote, but all the vegetables are locally grown, and delicious: the product of ample sunshine, mineral rich soil, and just sufficient moisture.

All markets have some arrangement for checking weights and hearing complaints. The official in charge of these matters at Arrecife is forever stalking between the stalls, although few markets can be less in need of his discipline. But then Arrecife has a general weakness for policemen. It has no less than four full-time traffic police, one of whom, in white uniform, is always on duty where the main street meets the waterfront—the only possible intersection likely to offer traffic problems.

The police are Arrecife's self-appointed ambassadors. On my first visit, in 1960, I was constantly pursued by Emilio, a native of Hierro 'destined' as a Civil Guard to Lanzarote, who by following BBC courses had taught himself a correct and fluent, if sometimes unusual English, and was always anxious for the opportunity to practise it. He has now been 'destined' elsewhere, and his place as linguist-in-chief has been taken by Heraclio Niz, the head of the traffic police, who races round the town on a motor cycle which is almost lost to view beneath his immense body.

Let not his size, nor the fact that he is everywhere referred to as *el pollo*, the chicken, make you under-estimate his character. Not fat, but muscle covers that mighty frame, and *el pollo*, far from implying any tenderness of flesh or spirit, is the title given to the champion of a team of Canary wrestlers. Lanzarote numbers four such teams, of which naturally the team of Arrecife is usually most successful; so that Heraclio Niz, as 'Pollo de Arrecife,' is the strongest man on the island.

On his suggestion I attended a match at the village of Tao between the teams of Tao and of Máguez. Each contained a dozen wrestlers ranging in age from about seventeen to thirty-five, wearing rather wide, rolled-up shorts with loose fitting, deep-necked shirts of an attractive cut I have only seen elsewhere on Breton fishermen.

Even before play began I sensed that I had stepped back into an earlier Lanzarote. For this unique style of wrestling has come down from native times. With Heraclio Niz beside me giving a running commentary I was soon able to follow the match, which consisted of individual encounters within a framework of team spirit.

Over a loudspeaker the referee announced the names of the next pair of contestants, who then circled each other for a few moments in the 'ring' left free in the centre of the threshing floor or farmyard where we all sat or stood. Their object was to force any part of their opponent's body to the ground, and the sides of the wide shorts seemed to be the favourite points for gripping.

The tense attention and vociferous encouragement of the two or three hundred *aficionados* present showed that this had as many subtleties as any other sport. Some of the bouts lasted seven or eight minutes, and the eventual triumph of the Tao or the Máguez protagonist would have his supporters on their toes, with the keenest amongst them throwing him *duros* (coins of five pesetas).

The permutations of pairing were neither haphazard nor followed a rigid pattern. Instead, the referee seemed to be fixing each wrestler's personal handicap as he went along. Only the best on either side were fit to measure up to the *pollo* or the *artista* of the other. (The 'Artist' is the title given to the runner-up of the 'Chicken'.) I have never seen a sport at once so healthy and so safe played with such good nature by such clean-limbed young men.

Arrecife's team is likely to become relatively even stronger as the years go by. For the easy communications have led to a progressive depopulation of the countryside as more and more people have left the hard and unrewarding land to establish themselves in the capital. This tendency for the head to grow at the expense of the body is to be found in all the islands, and indeed in all islands everywhere. In the Shetlands, for example, where the total population has dropped from 32,000 after the First World War to little more than half that figure today, that of Lerwick, the capital, has risen from 4,000 to 7,000. But Lanzarote is an extreme case. Arrecife now holds no less than 20,500 of the 44,000 inhabitants of Lanzarote. It is time that we set out to explore this harsh hinterland whose conditions have led to such a massive exodus.

You will be told that the island can be visited in two all day excursions: one to the south, and one to the north. Although these are bound to miss certain places, they have the merit of showing as much as possible to those short of time. It is for these two excursions, moreover, that the excellent and well-informed taxi drivers of Arrecife quote an inclusive price (per taxi, not per person: so if you number less than four find other congenial visitors to fill up the seats). So I shall follow their routes myself, recommending digressions from them for those with time to spare, or with their own transport.

Lanzarote

On my last visit I was lucky enough to have my own transport, but I soon found that Lanzarote's low altitudes and good roads had their own dangers. It was all too easy to lose one's way once out of sight of the sea. For there were no signposts at the cross-roads, and few people about from whom to ask the way. Moreover all the central region from a few miles to the west of Arrecife appears a desert—a black desert—and the unfamiliarity of the landscape makes it seem even more featureless than it is.

Lunar is the adjective always used to describe Lanzarote, and it is appropriate whether applied to the great lava field of the eighteenth century, or to these unending dust-filled craters, each about ten feet in diameter, and each separated from the next by a low wall of lava stones. But there is a non-lunar regularity about them. Nature's furnaces have created the raw materials of this landscape, but man has rearranged them.

We are in fact witnessing a most sophisticated method of farm-ing. At the centre of each crater grows a single vine. Its green does little to relieve the monotony of the black desert, for it is often invisible from a distance, the sides of each crater sloping down to perhaps five feet below its rim. The vine appears to be growing straight from the charcoal-grey volcanic dust; but in reality it has been planted in just sufficient ordinary soil, specially placed there, to cover its roots. This soil has then been deliberately covered with the volcanic ash. Deliberately, for it is this ash, itself useless, which has the property of distilling each night the dew which is the only moisture the vine receives.

On hearing of this for the first time I wondered if there could be much dew on an island where it hardly ever rains. But since then I have spent nights in various parts of Lanzarote in my motor caravan. I have awoken to condensation on the outside of my windows. The damp air has struck me as I emerged from the bar in Teguise where I had spent the evening. Most palpable proof of all, I have driven through a cloud over the Cuesta de los Valles on the interior road to Haría. I know now that there is plenty of moisture in the air, as there ought to be in a small low island with an abundance of sunshine to produce evaporation from the sur-rounding ocean.

Lanzarote

The property of the volcanic dust in absorbing this moisture is made use of in other parts of Lanzarote, and to a lesser degree in Fuerteventura, in a more extensive way. Whole fields of perfectly good—but waterless—soil are covered with an inch or so of ash, and thus are grown several other crops, and in particular the excellent onions for which Lanzarote has made a name and a considerable trade.

It is the vine, however, which has called forth most ingenuity. In the first place it grows on land which would otherwise serve no purpose whatsoever. In the second place the walls and side of the crater protect the plant from wind and sand. And in the third place the half-buried position of the vine reduces the sun's 'angle of incidence,' so that it is in shadow for a longer period than if it were growing on the level. It has been calculated that one hour more each day of direct exposure to the sun would often be enough to kill a vine.

Sophistication is indeed the word to describe Lanzarote's farming techniques. But it is the sophistication of special solutions lovingly found for particular problems. These techniques require hard work, and will not lend themselves to mechanization. So the drift to Arrecife—and beyond Arrecife to Las Palmas—continues.

Let us hope, however, that some wine will always be produced in Lanzarote. Due to the small amount of moisture it has received it has a high alcoholic content—sometimes as much as 20 per cent. By far the greatest amount produced is white. I normally prefer red, and have a deep distrust of 'volcanic' wines since the most explosive headache of my life the morning after drinking a bottle of *vino di Vesuvio* at Pompeii. Nevertheless the white 'volcanic' wine of Lanzarote brings back happy memories: many happy memories.

I suppose that I was lucky. The Peninsular Spaniard returning from a visit to the Canaries will tell you 'Everything is cheaper there . . . except the wine. That is very expensive. It costs fifteen pesetas a litre.' We may not regard 9p a bottle as so excessive, or even jib at the twenty-five pesetas a litre normally charged for the locally produced wines of Gran Canaria and Tenerife. But always out for a bargain, I was interested when the young man from whose newly opened store in Arrecife I used to buy my groceries asked only eight pesetas for a litre of the deep cinnamon coloured wine which he tapped from the huge barrel standing like a piece of prestige furniture just inside the door. It came, he told me, from his own vineyard at La Geria.

I found it delicious, whether taken as an *apéritif* or at table. More important, my aunt, to whom red wine is anathema, and who is highly selective even in regard to white, sternly pronounced it palatable as she and my mother sipped a glass on their private terrace at the *Parador*. The next stage of their winter abroad was to be two months in a furnished flat at Los Cristianos in Tenerife, and I saw the opportunity of a saving in an important item of our housekeeping budget. When my motor caravan was swung on board a few days later en route for Santa Cruz its water tanks were temporarily adapted to another use. I was personally exporting no less than fifteen gallons of wine from Lanzarote.

Having allowed my aunt a brief appearance, I cannot forbear repeating her comment as we drove south through the black vineyards.

'At last I know what to do with all that coke dust,' she exclaimed. 'I must write to my gardener and tell him to spread it around the kitchen garden.'

At Uga the road we have followed through the vineyards centred on La Geria meets the road which runs nearer the coast from Arrecife past the airport. From here too a byroad leads up a narrow valley in the southern hills to the hamlet of Femés, where stood the first cathedral of the Canaries: San Marcial de Rubicón.

The name of Rubicón survives today as that of the southern peninsula of the island, a waterless and infertile desert which has more in common with the northern tip of Fuerteventura than with the rest of Lanzarote. Yet it was here that Béthencourt chose for the first permanent European settlement. Here stood that 'castle of Rubicón' which features so largely in the account of Boutier and le Verrier. In those days the southern coast, sheltered from the dangerous winds which have prevented a single important port from developing on the west coast of any of the islands, was the natural gateway to one of the most fertile parts of Lanzarote. We enter this region immediately after leaving the next village, Yaiza, whose square houses stand unnaturally white against the dark country beyond.

Dark indeed! Here no half-buried vines hint at a fertility long since forgotten. These plains of black rock are not volcanic dust but lava itself, fantastically twisted into the shapes it had assumed at the moment it began to cool. The *canarios* have a word for this landscape: *malpais*, badland, land useless for cultivation or even for the sparsest of grazing. But most *malpais* has been colonized by plants of some kind. Even here in Lanzarote I have spent a long lunch hour gazing in fascination at the different species—some old friends from the sand-dunes of boyhood, some recognizable from rock gardens, and some purely Canary—which had established themselves in the *malpais* around the Cueva de los Verdes. But that lava has been inviting erosion and collecting dust for a comparatively long time. This, beyond Yaiza, belongs geologically to yesterday, and looks much as it did 230 years ago, when the last great eruption in the islands ended.

There have been lesser eruptions since, as in 1909 in Tenerife and in 1949 in La Palma. More serious was another in this same district of Lanzarote in 1824. But it is above all to the events of 1730 to 1736 that *canarios* look back when they speak with respect of the powers beneath their feet. There seems to have been little or no loss of human life. People had ample warning of when their homes were in danger, and the destruction went on for so long that it must have become accepted as part of everyday life. This is perhaps one reason why so little direct contemporary record has survived.

At first some of those affected took temporary shelter, with their goats and pigs and hens, over in Fuerteventura. Later many left Lanzarote forever, as others had left after the Moroccan raids of a century and a half earlier, and as others again were to leave during the great droughts of a century and a half later. For by then their homes had irrevocably disappeared. Ten *lugares* or hamlets were destroyed directly by the flow of lava, and thirteen more by the equally merciless 'rain of stones' reported by Bishop Davila of Las Palmas in an account which made me think of Churchill's heartening boast at the height of the blitz that it would take ten years at that rate to knock down half London, after which 'it would be slower'.

London's enemy, though equally infernal, was in the last resort mortal. But Lanzarote's enemy lives on, though dormant. Dormant not as the slumbering giants who are the vast majority of Canary volcanoes, nor even as the lighter sleeping Teide. Timanfaya, the ancient native name by which this destroyer is known, is but fitfully dozing, and those who approach him closely will realize that he lies only just below the level of consciousness.

The approach has been well organized, and contains two notable experiences. One consists in leaving the road to climb by camel a slippery forty-five degree mountain of volcanic dust which would not seem out of place amongst the slag heaps of a mining landscape. But the view from the rest-house at the top, over hundreds of spent volcanoes, great and small, belongs to Lanzarote alone—or perhaps to the moon. The riders, two to a camel, are strapped into their seats, which are suspended from either side of a framework fitting over the animal's hump. The outside passenger has the uncomfortable illusion of swinging out over space. He need not fear. The camel driver, with whom arrangements for this expedition must be made before leaving Arrecife (and will have been made by the taxi-driver on an all-in excursion), will be near at hand.

The other experience takes place at the point known as the Islote de Hilario, where the earth itself may be likened to the embers of a great bonfire. For here, just as in the ashes of a camp fire, eggs can be boiled and potatoes roasted by burying them a few inches in the soil; and straw placed in a rather deeper hole can soon be kindled into flame. It was all delightfully informal and do-it-yourself on my own visit there in 1960; but since then, I am told, things have been tidied up, and all the facilities provided for an almost Californian barbecue.

The most impressive tribute to the terror inspired by the Fire Mountains lies on the northern edge of the great black desert. Exactly on the edge. It is a cross where Our Lady of the Sorrows appeared and commanded the advancing lava to halt. And there, at the edge of the fields miraculously saved, the hamlet of Mancha

Blanca built a church dedicated to the Virgin de los Dolores, who has now become the patroness of the whole island, protecting not only her fields from fire but also her ships out at sea.

Before turning north to the heart of the Fire Mountains the taxi generally continues due west, still across the lava, to El Golfo, a pale-green lagoon cupped in a half-crater only a stone's throw from the breakers of the west coast. As in the case of the greater El Golfo on the west coast of Hierro, these breakers have undermined the other half of the crater wall, but enough survives to leave this pool isolated from the ocean. As it is usually here that one stops to eat a picnic lunch, it is an ideal spot for a midday swim, to see for oneself what truth there is in the claim that it contains more salt than the Dead Sea. My own buoyancy seemed neither greater nor less than usual.

Three miles south along the coast, but thrice the distance by road, is a much larger and equally bitter lake, Janubio, from which the salt is extracted by evaporation. There are many such *salinas* throughout the islands, for salt is their oldest industry. Here in Lanzarote there is another at El Charco four miles north of Arrecife, and another again on the mainland opposite Graciosa. The coarse salt which they produce is not intended for domestic use, but for preserving fish.

The standard excursion to the south goes no further than Janubio, but all who can should push on across the desolate plain of Rubicón to Playa Blanca, the poverty-stricken village of the far south, with its magnificent views across the straits called the Bocaina towards the islet of Lobos and the equally poverty-stricken northern tip of Fuerteventura. Prosperity of a sort may be on the way: here, as at Corralejo opposite, plots for villas were already being laid out in 1966. Their water supply will presumably come by lorry from Arrecife, which is at least more certain than that of Corralejo, which is to be delivered by boat from Las Palmas!

There have been a few forerunners of the crowds to come: a lone Austrian who pitched his solitary tent at the Punta de Papagayo itself, seven miles beyond nowhere; and the charming English couple I ran into on their arrival in Las Palmas, who own a house in Playa Blanca described by the villagers as '*la casa del embajador*'.

A couple of miles to the east of Playa Blanca a promontory is commanded by a circular tower called the Torre del Aguila. It was erected, as a plaque tells us, in 1778, and not as some guidebooks claim by Béthencourt. But before turning north again we may spare him another thought, for his castle of Rubicón,[1] protecting the natives of Lanzarote and Fuerteventura from slave raiders, as well as dominating them, did stand not far from here. Despite his rough and ready methods he was perhaps, like an earlier Norman conqueror, King William I of England, on the whole a 'good thing'.

The other standard excursion, that to the north of the island, generally starts with a visit to Teguise, which deserves a closer look and will be described later on. It then runs up the steep Cuesta de los Valles, which in conjunction with the narrowing of the island at this point makes the northern part of Lanzarote something of a world on its own. The commercial centre of this region is Haría, a large village set amidst palm trees in a green valley.

The self-sufficiency of this isolated area was brought home to me when at Máguez, the next village, I called on a friend I had met at the wrestling match over at Tao, to which as a keen supporter he had accompanied the Máguez team. After some years working in a Las Palmas establishment making 'mosaics' or tiles—which in the Canary climate take the place of carpets, linoleum, parquet, and every other type of floor covering—he had decided to set up a one man mosaic works in his own village.

'I was sure of enough work to keep me busy,' he told me as he showed me over his tiny factory, with its moulds, mixers, kiln, pigments, and ample supplies of British Portland Cement. 'Because although there were already two mosaicists in Lanzarote, there was none here in the north. All the business from Haría to Orzola, and over in Graciosa, has fallen automatically into my hands.'

He decided to celebrate my visit by taking the afternoon off, and together with another friend we drove down to the tiny fishing village of Orzola. There we ate fish and drank a good deal of Lanzarote wine, gossiping to the boatmen who arrived with one of Don Jorge Toledo's ships from Graciosa. We became steadily

[1] The foundations of this fortress were located in 1960 in the Barranco de los Pozos de San Marcial, near the abandoned village of Papagayo.

merrier over further drinks at Yé, and the evening ended in a golden haze at the casino or social club back in Máguez.

I was more sober, and would advise others who make the trip to be more sober, on the day that I drove beyond all these places to the far northern headland, to enjoy from La Batería a magnificent view over all the smaller islands, that microcosm of the Canaries which has been christened *el archipiélago menor*.

The two natural curiosities of this area lie close together near the east coast, approached by a lonely track over long exposed lava. But volcanic pressures here were in their time quite as intense as any at the other end of the island; and to escape from beneath the lava filling a dry river bed the exploding gases forced their way through a mile long tunnel called the Cueva de los Verdes. This was a refuge from Barbary raids three hundred years ago, and is today open to those accompanied by the excellent and essential guides provided by the Cabildo Insular. With a total of four miles of galleries it is the longest known volcanic cave in existence.

The Jameos de Agua, a much shorter cavern nearer the sea, was formed in a rather different way. The waters of the Atlantic, rushing into this molten fissure, built up such a head of steam that they blew off the stone 'cork' which can still be seen near the entrance. The salt water remained as a still lagoon, which can be approached down steps from two separate directions.

I first approached it from the landward side, hoping to see those 'blind monks in the white habit of St. Dominic' as the small sightless crab found here, the distinct species *Munidopsis polimorpha*, has been called. But I was alone, and the sudden contrast of the cool dark cavern with the glaring sunshine above was a little weird.

I was therefore psychologically half prepared for the uncanny sounds which presently began to drift over the water and to echo and re-echo round the walls. The music of the spheres perhaps? I would have been only moderately surprised had Orpheus himself floated towards me on Charon's skiff. A full three minutes passed before the wandering notes had re-formed themselves to emerge as 'The Blue Danube'. Whereupon I climbed back up, and walking round to the main entrance found it in process of being transformed into an exotic and unusual nightclub, due to be opened the following month. Through loudspeakers the Strauss LP rang round a dozen cunningly contrived private corners, with rustic chairs and tables, and cute lava ornaments. I felt ashamed at my first reactions to the sounds.

My shame was unnecessary, for I was not the only dupe. There in a long white row, four or five deep at the edge of the pool, acutely sensitive to sound despite their blindness, were massed all the representatives of the species *Munidopsis polimorpha*.

Two places on the north coast, although included in neither of the standard excursions, merit a visit by those with time to spare. One is the fine beach of Famara, facing the steep cliffs formed by the high ground we climbed on our way to Haría and to La Batería. At the adjoining fishing village of La Caleta I saw the catch being weighed on a home-made balance, a series of stones serving as weights. These people live by fish alone, for nothing will grow on the surrounding *malpais*, of which a large section has recently been purchased by a French syndicate for some £30,000.

The other is the island marked on some maps a mile or so to the east of the hamlet called La Santa. Drawn there by curiosity I found only a long narrow inlet, bending round on itself for half a mile. The sun beat down, but I was unwilling, all on my own, to face the mighty rollers at the end of their journey from America. Then I saw a man, dark and tattered like most of the Canary fisher folk and much of the Canary coastline, walking along collecting something amongst the rocks.

'You will be quite safe swimming here,' he said, taking me to a widening of the inlet. He went on to tell me that at high tides the inlet connected with the ocean at both ends, so that for a few hours each year the island really was an island.

'A lot of fish come in with the tide. And as it starts to ebb we dam both ends, and place in the water the juice of a plant we gather on the hillsides. This makes them float unconscious to the surface, where we simply gather them up. You won't have heard of this and it's rather hard to explain' he concluded apologetically.

But I had heard about it. Viera y Clavijo, the great historian of the islands, described exactly this use of the milky sap of the *cardón* by the natives before the conquest.

Lanzarote

To reach both these points we have to pass through Teguise, and it is time that we at last visited the old capital. From the sixteenth-century castle of Guanapay above the town we can see how it sits in the saddle of the island, midway between the oceans to north-west and south-east, and between the mountains to north-east and south-west. By night it seems quieter than Máguez or Tao, perhaps due to the wide streets and empty spaces over which its fifteen hundred souls are spread. But to the *conejos*[1] it remains *la Villa*, the royal town which Arrecife, *el puerto*, will never be.

For this was the very first of all those capitals of conquistadores, from La Laguna in Tenerife to Lima in Peru, where in church and in convent the God of the newcomers received on glittering altars the worship of those who had been at once conquered and converted. Two of the conventual churches, San Francisco and Santo Domingo, can be visited when one has located the parish sacristan. One's memory of them, as of the whole town, is of an echoing emptiness.

It was no doubt a slightly busier place in 1726, four years before the great eruption of Tinamfaya, when there was born here José Clavijo y Fajardo, of a well respected Canary family. He left the islands in 1745 and in 1763 his ability secured him a post in the Royal Archives, which he lost only the following year after a scandal which has made his name famous.

In the eighteenth century, as today, any *francesa* was sure of a success in Spain, especially if she lived up to the reputation which French girls have unjustifiably acquired abroad. Trading on this reputation the sister of the French playwright Beaumarchais came to Madrid and lived well off her wits. Beaumarchais himself, visiting the Spanish capital on equally unscrupulous business, extracted at pistol-point a promise to marry his sister from Clavijo, who was only one of her many men friends. Adding insult to injury, he based his drama *Eugenia* on the incident, and gave an embroidered account of it in his *Fragment of my journey to Spain*, which in turn inspired Goethe's still more fictional work *Clavigo*.

Perhaps after all Teguise represents a happier blending of two

[1] Literally 'rabbits', the name always given to inhabitants of Lanzarote. See Appendix 5: Vital Statistics.

races than the great cities of Latin America. In a long shed at the edge of one of those empty spaces which may once have been squares the friendly proprietor will pick from amongst the half completed guitars and mandolins a small instrument which might at first seem like a pocket edition of them. It is the *timple*, the *canario*'s own favourite accompaniment. It may have originated in Lanzarote, and it is certainly here in Teguise that the best examples are still made.

Then the very name Teguise is that of the daughter of the last native king of the island. She became the wife of Maciot de Béthencourt, nephew and successor of the conqueror. Did Aztec or Inca princesses become consorts of the viceroys?

Her father was a remarkable man, welcoming the newcomers in a statesmanlike way, never breaking his word though they so often broke theirs, and twice escaping single-handed from captivity. His mother, too, had been a remarkable woman, surviving a trial by ordeal which killed two others. The trial was to discover whether she was the legitimate daughter of her father, the legendary Zonzamas, or the daughter of a visiting Castilian nobleman who perhaps received rather more than bread and board from his royal host.

But to meditate on the lost kingdom of *Tite-roy-gatra*—which may have been a queendom if we accept the theory of matriarchy which has been advanced with regard to the eastern islands—we must go to those lonely stones hidden in the plain behind Arrecife, stones which go by the name of the Castillo de Zonzamas. Here, at Teguise, let us end our account of Lanzarote where we began, with Jean de Béthencourt.

He was in the islands a total of less than three years, and never returned to them after his final departure at the end of 1405, dying childless twenty years later in a Normandy which had just been conquered by the English. As Viera y Clavijo put it: 'He saw his country in the same conflict in which he had placed the kings of the Canaries.'

The three islands which he conquered: Lanzarote, Fuerteventura and Hierro, were the easiest and in many ways the least important, and even this reduced inheritance was sold and resold by his nephew and successor. (The claim made in *Le Canarien* and repeated by Viera y Clavijo that he also conquered Gomera has been shown to be false; but Béthencourt may have thought that he had extracted some token submission from the fierce inhabitants of that precipitous isle.) Yet Maciot de Béthencourt seems to have remained in and around the Canaries for the rest of his life, and a descendant of his, another Maciot, moved over to Gran Canaria when it was conquered and there married another native princess, Luisa Guanarteme, a niece of the ruler of Telde.

It was this second Maciot who sent his son Andrés de Betancor (note the change in spelling) to visit his distant cousin at the old family home in Normandy in 1501. This cousin, Jean V de Béthencourt, was descended from another nephew of the conqueror, and had forgotten that he even had any relatives in the Canaries. But he had the account of the conquest written by Boutier and le Verrier, and proudly sent off to Maciot II a copy, edited and embellished—presumably by himself—in which the role of Gadifer de la Salle is significantly played down. (See footnote, page 42.)

In the following century the Béthencourts of Normandy died out, and the name ceased to exist in France itself. It was with surprise and interest, therefore, that Professor Cioranescu of La Laguna University learnt that a M. de Béthencourt had been appointed as Minister of Information and Tourism in the Government of M. Mendès-France. But on calling on him in the hope of bringing to light further documents of early Canary history he discovered that the Minister was descended from *canarios* re-established in France centuries after the original Norman baron had gone south.

For by now the Béthencourts, Betancors and Betancourts are in every island of the archipelago and in every state of Latin America (one was recently President of Venezuela). As Bettencourts and Bittencourts they have made their way to Madeira, Portugal and Brazil. Travelling round the Canaries you will buy food from Béthencourt grocers, and be driven by Béthencourt taxi-drivers. If you buy a plot for a bungalow, the chances are that it will be sold to you by a Béthencourt landowner.

It has been explained that not all are necessarily descendants in

7. Lanzarote: church at Tias

8. Lanzarote: San Gabriel Castle, Arrecife (p. 48)

10. Gran Canaria: the tangled landscape of the Cumbre seen from the Cruz de Tejeda. The monolith on the skyline is the Roque Nublo (pp. 103–104)

9. Gran Canaria: view from the farm in the crater of Bandama up towards the peak from which visitors look down (p. 96)

11. Gran Canaria: stallholder with assorted wares in Las Palmas market

the male line of the conqueror or of his family. In Castile until a century ago people adopted whichever parent's name they wished —and, of course, both parents' names are still given in formal documents. And as amongst the negroes of America, natives and slaves often adopted the name of their godfather or master.

Some such explanation is needed, for otherwise the conqueror must have spent a very busy three years indeed. Today three out of every two hundred *canarios* bear his surname. In Lanzarote alone the Béthencourts in 1951 numbered 669 out of 16,194 adults, or more than 4 per cent of the population.

A friend's remark: 'Lanzarote is now the *Costa Smeralda* of the Canaries', sums up the changes which have taken place in five years. They have been along the lines I indicated. The night club at Jameos de Agua is now in regular operation. The coastline south of Arrecife is in full development.

But the development is unexpectedly discreet. Unlike larger and more populous isles to the west, Lanzarote has risen to the challenge of 'urbanisation' under the inspiration of one of her own sons. He is the painter César Manrique, who has created for Lanzarote an architectural idiom such as half a century ago Néstor de la Torre created for Gran Canaria.

As befits the island for which it is designed, Manrique's idiom is more austere, more cubist in its basic shapes. Its supreme model is his own home, built symbolically atop a lava-flow. Not only the house, but lamps, ornaments, furniture and pictures have all been designed or executed by the artist himself. But his ideas infuse also all the new building on Lanzarote, whose Cabildo Insular wisely listens to his views before passing development plans.

The only one of his achievements which is not universally appreciated is his monument to the Lanzarote peasant. But the fast-disappearing countryfolk of this volcanic isle certainly deserved commemoration; and who better than a fellow *lanzaroteño* to provide it?

❧ 3 ❧

Fuerteventura

It is hard to get a balanced opinion on Fuerteventura. Everyone reacts to it with violence. Those who like it praise the Biblical quality of its dry, uncompromising hills; the simple good nature of its few but worthy inhabitants; and its vast empty beaches, their sands golden like few others in the Canaries. Those who dislike it complain of the shortage of water; of the lack of every civilized amenity; of a rough earthy people as primitive as the land they live in; of dust and of boredom.

There is something to be said for both views, and both demand violent expression. For Fuerteventura is itself violent. As the boat leaves Arrecife behind, the strange lunar landscape of Lanzarote assumes in retrospect an almost domestic cosiness by comparison with the harsh red mountains rearing up ahead. Everything in Fuerteventura is on a bigger scale. It is almost three times the size of Lanzarote (if its area were 2 per cent greater it would exceed Tenerife and would be the largest island in the archipelago), has even less rainfall, lies even nearer to Africa—and numbers only half the population. It has therefore often been described as an extension of the Sahara desert. Certainly the flat brown plains, the large number of camels[1] (here bred for export to the other islands) and the herds of goats which until recently gave the capital the name of Puerto Cabras (Goat Port) can all be found over in the Rio de Oro.

It is these physical resemblances to Africa, but to an Africa with no diseases, no snakes, no wild animals, no race problems, and no anti-colonialism, which added to the beaches have in the last few

[1] Which I propose to continue calling them throughout this book, although technically they are dromedaries.

years attracted a few dozen immigrants to Fuerteventura, the first reversal of a tide of emigration which over the centuries has carried countless thousands of *maioreros*[1] to the New World. As recently a ten years ago Herr Winter, the German who between the wars had settled down to farm in the southern peninsula of Jandía, was widely regarded as eccentric.

There is nothing eccentric about the motives of the developers who have been moving in since 1960. I would not myself choose to invest in an island which 'imports water and exports stone,' but I am no judge of real estate. Already artesian wells[2] are being sunk in the south, and in time a distillation plant, as in Lanzarote, may end the nightmare dependence of some developments on the water ship from Las Palmas. And Fuerteventura is already quite an easy place to get to. It has an airfield. And it is the only island at which the mail steamers call at two distinct ports.

Puerto del Rosario, as the capital has been grandiloquently renamed, is the port at which we arrive from Arrecife. Although a third of the island's population now live there, it is of recent growth, for in 1790 not a single house stood on this bay. Good beaches are within easy reach, and until recently it had the only possible hotel accommodation in Fuerteventura.

A good road runs inland, and then down the centre of the island through the villages of Casillas del Angel, La Antigua and Tuineje. The territory of Tuineje includes much of the south coast, where one of its dependent hamlets is now more important than the village itself. This is Gran Tarajal, where this main road down the centre ends, running the last mile or two through a valley filled with *tarajal* (the Canary tamarisk), from which this second port of Fuerteventura derives its name.

This accounts for the Tarajal, but not for the Gran. The only thing which is great about Gran Tarajal is its unattractiveness. I am not easily bored, nor depressed, and on Spanish soil hardly

[1] See Appendix 5: Vital Statistics.

[2] The water of many of Fuerteventura's wells is slightly saline, and therefore unsuitable for bananas, although the island grows excellent tomatoes. After some years land irrigated with this water becomes too salty, and cultivation has to be moved.

ever. But on the two occasions I have been in Gran Tarajal I have been both, despite the fact that I have been in company. I dread to think what I would feel like there on my own, kicking my heels round those four or five mean streets as I waited for the boat to carry me away, or wandering from one to another of those terrible tatty bars, where all the dangerous looking characters of Fuerteventura seem to congregate.

But of course if I had twenty-four hours or more to spare I would be off down to Jandía, Fuerteventura's far south, which by ancient high-sprung taxis and modern Land-Rovers communicates with the outside world through Gran Tarajal, though administratively it belongs to the village of Pájara. The road runs fairly near the south coast, and then turns sharply north from ocean to ocean across the two mile isthmus which leads to Jandía. In doing so it follows a parallel course to the remains of a wall which has given this neck of land the name of the Istmo de la Pared.

Most authorities say that this was the wall which we know existed to separate the two native kingdoms into which Fuerteventura was divided. I have always been puzzled as to how the southern kingdom, wall or no wall, managed to survive if it was only a tenth the size of its northern neighbour; and also why, when Béthencourt and de la Salle landed in the north, they found themselves fighting both kings and their followers. I have now learnt that there are traces of many other walls in different parts of the island, and my guess would be that the frontier wall between the kingdoms lay farther north.

Great beaches border the coasts of Jandía: in the north that of Barlovento to windward, and in the south that of Sotavento to leeward. Between them lies the massif which culminates in the Pico de la Zarza, at 2,700 feet the highest point of the island. The tiny centres of habitation, of which the most remote is the lighthouse at the far western promontory, are supplied with religious services and primary education at Morro Jable. And in the lonely Valle de los Mosquitos of this lonely peninsula, and there alone, grows the cactus-like *euphorbia handiensi*, a *cardón* more than three feet high.

The swimming off Jandía is good. But the underwater fishing

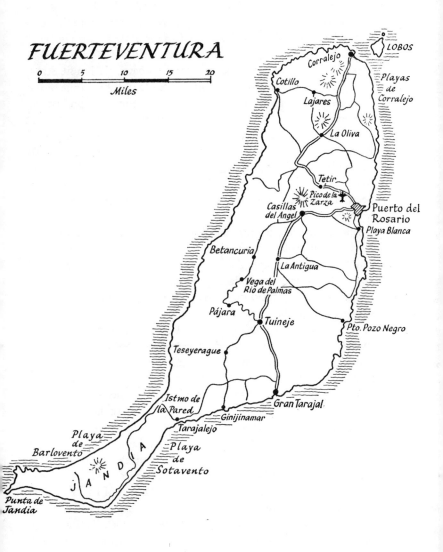

FUERTEVENTURA

0 5 10 15 20
Miles

LOBOS

Corralejo

Playas
de
Corralejo

Cotillo

Lajares

La Oliva

Tetir

Pico de la
Zarza

Casillas
del Angel

Puerto del
Rosario

Playa Blanca

Betancuria

La Antigua

Vega del
Rio de Palmas

Pájara

Tuineje

Pto. Pozo Negro

Teseyerague

Istmo de
la Pared

Gran Tarajal

Ginijinamar

Tarajalejo

Playa
de
Barlovento

Playa
de
Sotavento

J A N D I A

Punta de
Jandia

for which Fuerteventura has become famous is best enjoyed from the other end of the island, where fish abound in the shallow straits isolating the island of Lobos. This derives its name from the incident when Gadifer de la Salle was left stranded there when he went hunting seals, *lobos marinos*, to provide the expedition with sealskin shoes. At the fishing village of Corralejo particularly fine straw hats are woven, following a tradition already old at the time of the conquest, to judge from woven rushwork found at prehistoric sites in perfect preservation in the dry climate.

Another memory of the Normans is recalled by their castle of Rico Roque near Cotillo, ten miles to the west of Corralejo. To reach it we must cross some of the desolate *malpais* which covers much of the north, passing at Lajares windmills which might have been transported from the almost equally lonely plains of La Mancha in Castile.

But the most eloquent survival of the early years of the conquest lies in a high valley deep in the western hills. Fom Gran Tarajal it can be reached through Tuineje and Pájara, where the church has an unusual carved stone façade, and on through the oddly lush sounding Vega del Rio de Palmas. From the capital on the other hand the route bears right after Casillas del Angel, and climbs steeply to give magnificent views. These are the oldest hills of Fuerteventura, the sole remains of an ancient cordillera which, had it not ages ago collapsed into the sea, would have made this the largest island and perhaps distilled for it a little more rain.

And now below us lies the village which would still perpetuate Béthencourt's name if no man bore it. Betancuria is the smallest *municipio* in the island, with the least cultivable ground, but like Teguise in Lanzarote it was the capital in the days when the flat eastern coastlands stood open to Barbary raiders—who nevertheless penetrated here in 1593, and burnt the church of Santa María. Even rebuilt it is the most important monument of the island. Its sacristy has a fine painted ceiling, and there are murals depicting scenes from the life of the Virgin, in one of which the figures of King Ferdinand and Queen Isabella can be seen in the background.

There is something violent about the loneliness of Betancuria. There is violence, too, in the very air of Fuerteventura, where from

Fuerteventura

November to April the central plains are visited by that strange tropical phenomenon, a wandering fireball called the *rayo en bola*. Whatever its attractions today for back-to-nature sun lovers, it has certainly never been regarded as a desirable place of residence by Spanish governments. As recently as 1962 Gil Robles, the right wing and Catholic politician, who had foolishly attended a conference of Spanish opposition leaders at Munich, was on his return home politely offered the choice of immediate exile abroad, or Fuerteventura. In choosing Fuerteventura he was continuing an illustrious tradition, for it has often served as a place of free and easy detention for top people—much as did the Aeolian Islands for leading Romans under the early Empire.

These exiles were in fact merely being insula-ted. In making this pun I am not being facetious, but simply translating so far as I may the play of words made by the most distinguished of these exiles. For he described his enforced arrival at Puerto Cabras on 12th March 1924 as *a-isla-miento* (*aislamiento* means isolation, and *isla* means island). And it was hardly possible to accuse of facetiousness the Rector of Salamanca University, Spain's Oxford and Cambridge rolled into one: Don Miguel Unamuno.

In fact he took himself very seriously. The military directory of General Primo de Rivera, which had decreed his *a-isla-miento* after he had attacked it in an Argentine newspaper and in a speech at Bilbao, deliberately allowed him every possible opportunity of escape on his journey there, including eight days of unsupervised freedom in Las Palmas. But it was dealing with a self-righteous martyr determined to offer himself to the lions.

So Unamuno took up residence in the island's only pension, the Hotel Fuerteventura, 'a humble lodging wedged between the prison and the church' as he put it. He was luckier than my mother and myself on our own first visit there in 1960. The Hotel Fuerteventura, then still the only place to stay, was entirely occupied by a congress of all the mining engineers of the province of Las Palmas. It was only with the greatest difficulty that I found two beds in a loft, separated by a tattered canvas curtain. Making our way there down a narrow passage we passed a stable, where the dim light of a hurricane lamp revealed a line of camels, and a man busy stuffing a couple of sacks with the straw from their stalls.

'Those,' said my mother, pointing to the sacks, 'will be our mattresses.' She was right.

Woken in the morning with a few valuable cupfuls of water for washing, we each in turn walked out to the *azotea* or terrace, to perform, like Bathsheba, our ablutions. Looking down, we found that we were wedged, not between church and prison, but just as significantly between a courtyard full of sheep and another courtyard full of goats. Gazing over the flat white rooftops towards the red mountains where Hollywood could have found the ideal location for a mammoth sacred epic, my mother declared, 'Never in my life have I felt, literally or metaphorically, more Biblical.'

The Hotel Fuerteventura has also its *azotea*, and Don Miguel imitated Bathsheba all too closely in using it to sunbathe in the nude. When, as might be expected, the neighbours complained to the proprietor, he replied, '*Yo no los miro. Que no me miren ellos a mí.*' 'I don't look at them. Let them not look at me.'

With this one exception his relations with the local inhabitants were excellent. The same craving for simplicity which had led to this incident made him temperamentally well-suited to life in Fuerteventura. He had always avoided wearing a tie, and here his dress was as simple as that of any *maiorero*, and his feet shod in the same canvas *alpargatas*.

We have already noted that he only brought three books on his journey south. They included, significantly, *The Divine Comedy* of Dante, another great exile. But he supplemented these by borrowings from the more cultured residents. Nor did he lose touch with these friends after his departure—for after four months he was prevailed upon to escape to France on the yacht of an admirer. Thus, in a letter written to one of these friends in 1936, the last year of his life, he recalls the villages which he used to visit on camel rides into the interior:

'How many times do I think that I would be better there, in Puerto de Cabras, or in La Oliva, or in Pájara, or in La Antigua, or in Betancuria . . . in Paris I am better informed perhaps of what is going on, but there, in the Island, I was informed of the realities.'

The letter reads like poetry. But then he was a poet, and as a poet could not but find inspiration in an island which he described as 'an oasis in the desert that is civilization'. Even lying naked on the *azotea* he was inspired to compose a sonnet which ran appropriately:

> '*Al sol de la verdad pongo desnuda mi alma . . .*'
> (In the sun of truth I lay out naked my soul.)

Accustomed as he was to the bare *meseta* around Salamanca, he was better able than most of us to grasp the essential, skeleton-like quality of this strange, violent island. Let the last words on it be his:

> '*Oh! Fuerteventurosa isla africana,*
> *sufrida y descarnada cual camello . . .*'

Though the biggest developments in Fuerteventura during the past five years have occurred at Corralejo in the far north and in Jandía in the far south, there are also plans for further 'urbanisations' along the east coast, and even on the west on the *Costa Pájara*, so called after the nearest village. Puerto del Rosario itself now boasts a government Parador. The road south from Gran Tarajal should be properly made up by 1973.

With its sparse, poor population, Fuerteventura had no valid local tradition of architecture to which this upsurge of building could conform. But empty spaces impose their own harmony. Just at present it is possible to enjoy a still primitive Jandía from the luxury of a hotel with all modern conveniences.

❧| 4 |❧

Gran Canaria

 W hy Gran Canaria? It is neither the biggest island, nor the highest, nor the most central, nor the most populous—all the distinctions of Tenerife. Yet it has given its name to the whole group, and has acquired the title 'great'.

Historically both words have a noble descent.[1] King Juba's expedition two thousand years ago named this island Canaria after a race of large dogs (*canes*) found there, dogs believed by some to be the ancestors of the *bardino* watchdogs of Fuerteventura. 'Gran' was added by Béthencourt's fellow conquistador Gadifer de la Salle, as a tribute to the courage of the inhabitants when he failed to conquer them.

And Gran Canaria, as we come to know her, deserves the name. Although her highest point is at 6,350 feet only just over half the height of Teide, this in itself gives the scenery of the smaller island a greater variety. For in Tenerife the eye can never escape the all-embracing surge upwards to the peak. But here the tangled central massif called the Cumbre, because it is much lower, is much less dominant. Other geographic regions, therefore: lesser hills, plains, and even a lagoon in the far south, are able to develop a personality of their own. Because of this variety Gran Canaria has been well named 'a continent in miniature'.

Only a tiny proportion of visitors ever discover the fulness of this variety. But no one ever visits Gran Canaria without learning

---

[1] The canary, the yellow songbird, derived its name from the islands —not the islands theirs from the bird. Seen in its native habitat, or for sale in cages in Las Palmas market, its colouring is much more subfusc than that of its domesticated cousins, with only a few greenish yellow feathers against a grey or brown background.

the other reason for its importance. For it possesses the largest city in the Canaries, and the busiest port in Spain.

Strictly speaking the city and the port are not the same thing. The deep anchorage of Puerto de la Luz lies, like all major Canary harbours, on the east coast, though only just so, sheltering in the lee of the bare hilly peninsula of La Isleta, known only to the military and to the souls of long gone aboriginals who there lie buried. Within living memory there was at least a suggestion of open country along the four mile road south to the capital, which had grown up around the camp fortified beside the palms by Juan Rejón the conquistador in 1478. Starting with the development of the Garden City in the last century, these four miles have now been continuously built up. Today only the name of a park and of a luxury hotel remind us that a solitary chapel of Santa Catalina once stood between the port and Las Palmas.

I have mentioned this distinction between *la ciudad* and *el puerto* only to abjure it. For myself, and for any visitor, Las Palmas is one: city, port, and now resort; from its ritziest hotels to its sleaziest bars; from the old quarter round the cathedral which already stood when Columbus passed this way, to the new constructions on Las Canteras beach which rise even as we watch them; at once typically Canary yet supremely cosmopolitan, the busy yet leisured metropolis of the mid-Atlantic.

It seems vast as our ship waits its turn to enter the harbour where, today as every day, forty other ships will drop anchor. And it will still feel vast a month later, when we have shop window gazed a dozen times down the length of Triana, and lingered over twice a dozen coffees in the Parque Santa Catalina three miles away.

Yet although almost two out of every three people in Gran Canaria, and indeed one in five in the entire archipelago live in Las Palmas, 270,000 would anywhere else be merely the population of a respectable provincial town. But Las Palmas is spread along the waterfront in a five-mile-long ribbon less than a mile in width, and is suffused with the cosmopolitan colour of a floating population which is renewed from month to month, from week to week, and even, in the case of the great liners and the cruise ships, from day to day.

Gran Canaria

It is from these last that most of us hear our first accounts of Las Palmas: vivid, vague, highly personal impressions of a few hours ashore on a Christmas cruise or on the way back from Australia.

'I didn't like Las Palmas. It was so dusty and tatty after the neatness and flowers of Madeira where we'd just come from.'

'Now that's where I'd choose for a honeymoon—Las Palmas. We'd left England in fog and ice, and there was this lovely golden beach covered with gorgeous Swedish girls in bikinis.'

'It was drizzling throughout the six hours we spent at Las Palmas. But it wouldn't have appealed to me if the sun had been shining. If there are two things I'd go a long way to avoid they're Scandinavian tourists and Indian shopkeepers.'

'I know where I'd settle if I didn't have to work for a living. Las Palmas. The climate's as good as the best South Africa or Australia has to offer. And the shopping's fabulous. They've got great supermarkets now, with everything you have at home, at practically the same prices, right down to New Zealand butter and Heinz Baked Beans. Then there are shops full of Japanese transistors and cameras with no purchase tax or import duty. And the drink! Gin and whisky at a pound a bottle!'

None of these views are wholly misleading. I have myself spent days in Las Palmas when I have been depressed by the dust, dampened by drizzle, or fascinated by the shops on Triana or by the shapes on Las Canteras. But the truest impression of a place is surely the memory of it which recurs most frequently; and for me this is of my first arrival, soon after landing, in the Parque Santa Catalina.

We reach it along the busy main road which cuts it off from the shipping offices on the waterfront—a long mile even as the crow flies from where our ship will have docked on the other side of the harbour. The sea is only three or four 'blocks' away in the other direction, for we are still on the isthmus of Guanarteme, which runs out to the peninsula of La Isleta, so that there is generally a breeze to temper the hot sunshine. We are glad of the palms and clumps of shrubs which justify giving the title of the park to what is really a vast tiled square.

Square in the sense of the Italian *piazza* rather than of the

GRAN CANARIA

Miles
0 1 2 3 4 5

LA ISLETA

Las Canteras Beach
Guanarteme
Isthmus
Puerto de la Luz
Las Alcaravaneras Beach
Las Palmas
Triana
Vegueta

Sardina
Montaña de Galdar
Galdar
El Roque
San Felipe

Guia
Cenobio de Valerón

Puerto de las Nieves
Agaete

Moya
Firgas
Arucas

Berrazales

Pine Forest of Tamadabh

Angostura
Teror Valley
Monte Coello
Santa Brigida
La Atalya
Tafira Baja
Tafira Alta
Bandama

Artenara

Las Lagunetas
San Mateo
Telde

Cruz de Tejeda
Tejeda
Bentaiga
Barranco de San Nicolás
Roque Nublo
Pozo de las Nieves
Cuatro Puertas
Gando Airport

San Nicolas

TIRAJANA
Santa Lucia
Ingenio
Agüimes

San Bartolomé de Tirajana

Mogán

Fataga

Arinaga

Puerto de Mogán

Juan Grande

Arguineguín

San Agustín

Maspalomas
Punta de Maspalomas

Gran Canaria

Spanish *plaza*, for it is for pedestrians only. But no *piazza* has half a dozen open-air cafés in regular use all the year round and for practically every hour of the twenty-four. Here, where the kiosks offer the day's news in a dozen tongues—for only in Las Palmas can the visitor to the islands purchase European newspapers on the day of their appearance—is the city's social hub. Here everybody sooner or later meets everyone else. Here, relaxing amidst the amenities of the world from whose rigours he has escaped, northern man experiences a specifically Canarian *douceur de vivre*.

Here at adjoining tables sit the palefaced visitors on a three hours' call and the bronzed pensioners who have settled in for the winter; the loud laughing emigrants to Australia and the sophisticated yacht owners on their way to the Caribbean; the Finns and the Swedes; the Danes and the Dutch; and even a few native *canarios*. Their faces wear relaxed, un-tense expressions, for the comings and goings in London and Stockholm, and even in Madrid, although so easy to follow, are a long way away.

Though escapists all, they have followed the orthodox routes here. The same cannot be said of certain other expatriates to be found in the Parque Santa Catalina. Their most extreme representatives when last I was there were young Germans, *wandervögel* of monstrous plumage who sat with long dishevelled locks and bizarre baggage in an unsavoury circle which other visitors carefully avoided. They were only the most conspicuous of a whole underworld of Las Palmas life, young people from the four corners of the earth who had come south for the same reasons but without the resources of older visitors, or who had been washed up in the Hesperides at the end of a latter day grand tour across Europe.

Some lived in cheap rooms and some slept on the beach. Their unofficial club was *El Avión* in the Calle Ripoche, the street running back from the centre of the Parque Santa Catalina. Meeting them there I found Bohemia, as usual, a land of frustration rather than of freedom. Many had hoped to find work, but only one capable young couple had been lucky: she as a nurse at the Queen Victoria English Hospital, and he teaching English for Berlitz.

I had come to the Canaries with three great advantages. I already knew them well. I had something to do. Above all, I had brought my motor caravan. It was with guilt at my good fortune that I would return from a breath-taking expedition to the Cumbre or to the far west of the island to find the same groups round the same tables in *El Avión*, eating the same dull meals which for all their cheapness were more expensive than the nourishing dishes which I cooked up for myself.

The life of the Calle Ripoche was the only Gran Canaria they would know, and that very basic English which serves as *lingua franca* at youth hostels and camping sites across five continents was the only language they would hear. Wintering in Las Palmas is cheaper than wintering in Manchester or Munich, but funds which are never replenished eventually dry up. He is in a very real sense consuming capital who starts to live on the sale of his blood to the hospital at 300 pesetas a litre. When a familiar face greeted me with a mixture of relief and of resignation I knew that its owner had thrown in the sponge and applied to his consul for repatriation. In his eyes I could see the steady job and the insurance stamp, and listening carefully I could faintly detect the distant sound of wedding bells.

I have described these failed escapists in some detail in order to emphasize the contrast with a much smaller, and in general older group who go south with equally exiguous resources, but who make a total success of the same unorthodox way of life. I remember meeting one of them as I was parked in a street running back from Las Canteras. He was a dapper little Englishman in his early fifties, in a light woollen shirt and knife-edge creased trousers, with a towel rolled neatly under his arm. The only difference between him and a thousand other men swimming in Las Palmas that day was that he looked more suitable and therefore smarter, without shapeless shorts or lily-white skin or sagging stomach.

'I hope you don't mind my saying so,' he remarked as he paused at the open door of my motor caravan, 'but you really have found the answer. An outfit like this would be ideal for me.'

'Come in and share the coffee I'm just making,' I said.

'No thanks: I haven't had lunch yet. But I'd love to step inside and see how everything works.'

And in return I learnt how he worked, or more precisely, how he had come to give up work. He had made the great decision four years earlier. 'But I wish I'd done so twenty years ago,' he added.

He still took jobs, but only odd jobs to suit himself, as and when he needed money. The previous winter had passed comfortably caretaking a closed hotel on the Costa Brava. From there he had made his way to Cannes, sure of being taken on as crew on one of the luxury yachts which only put to sea for the summer months. Twenty weeks' cruising off the French and Italian Rivieras at £15 a week had enabled him to save £300. So this winter he had come south, and was taking life easier still in the Canaries.

'Of course, I have to travel light,' he explained. 'This is made easier by following the sunshine. I have only one pair of shoes, two pairs of socks, two pairs of trousers, two shirts, one jacket, and a nylon raincoat. All my possessions fit into one small bag which swings easily from one shoulder. So if the worse comes to the worst I can always get from one place to another on my feet.'

'You look surprisingly smart on such a minute wardrobe.'

'When you've only a few things you have to keep them looking right. As soon as anything begins to wear out I throw it away. I only have room for what I really need. That goes for everything else too. Last week my landlady wanted to give me a silver cigarette case which had belonged to her husband. But I had to refuse it because it would have been that much extra weight to carry around, and I haven't the heart to flog something given me out of sheer kindness. What I miss most are books, which of course are the heaviest things of all. That's why your van appeals to me so much, although the upkeep of it would involve me in greater expense and therefore in more work. But it might almost be worth it, just to have somewhere of one's own to go to, and an encyclopaedia to consult whenever one wanted to find something out. Yes, books and the beach mean more to me than anything.'

He laughed to himself and went on: 'I can talk about these things to you, because you seem to be living in a rather similar way. This morning on Las Canteras I got talking to a nice English couple staying at the Metropol, who were sorry that their holiday was ending tomorrow. They wanted to know how long I was staying, and jumped when I told them until April or May. They asked if I was a millionaire, as surely no one else could lead such a life. But I assured them that any fool can do it.'

The truth is, however, that by no means every fool can do it. The little man sitting in my van had survived because he pursued the simple life with supreme efficiency, and because he had reduced his already simple tastes to well below the level of his slender means. His £300 savings represented a greater relative security than the salary of the £5,000 a year executive. Moreover he had thought out his position.

'To balance one's budget it is so much easier to reduce one's personal wants than to increase one's income. The end result is the same.'

His philosophy even embraced the ultimate problem.

'People say to me, "What happens if you're ill, all on your own, miles from anywhere?" Well, either you take the right medicine and lie up until you're better; or, if you become unconscious, someone finds you and fetches a doctor. And if they don't . . . well, its got to happen sometime, somewhere. You die, and that's that.'

The very air of Las Palmas is sympathetic to such a way of life. Where else would official recognition be given to an institution like the *Cabullón*? An acquaintance was recounting to me his life history.

'After the factory had closed down I wasn't sure what to do. Then, as I had a bit of capital saved, my brother-in-law invited me to go into partnership with him in the *Cabullón*. What? You've never heard of the *Cabullón*!'

He began to explain what it was. Soon I realized that I was talking to one of those characters, of whom we English are taught to be so suspicious, who board boats at big ports, selling dolls in local costume, cigarettes and watches, and who offer to change money and to initiate one into the night-life of the red light district. But here it seemed a job like any other, not merely recognized but institutionalized.

'Of course, I had to apply to the Port Authority for my card as a *cabullonero*, licensing me to go aboard ships and to trade. Buying is just as important for us as selling. Our profit margin comes, for example, from buying a transistor from a sailor off a Japanese whaler, and selling it to an American tourist on a cruise liner.'

He was a friendly soul. After I had bought him a drink he insisted on buying one for me. As we said goodbye I knew that for me dagoes had receded even further from Calais.

Las Canteras beach has already been mentioned so often that it is time we visited it, threading our way from the Parque Santa Catalina across a maze of streets which confuse because they just fail to follow an exact gridiron pattern.

A tiled promenade a mile and a half long borders the beach, and walking along it we are at once conscious of a subtle difference from other promenades we have known, at Blackpool, at Bournemouth, or at La Baule. Not only are the buildings lining the landward side insignificant in themselves, but we never even notice them. Here the beach is all.

A golden beach in islands where most beaches are black, it is never out of season; for the *canarios* themselves begin to swim as the last of the winter season tourists depart.[1] It has odd groups of rocks to give it interest as the tide slowly covers or reveals them: clean, glistening rocks like those of the sunset beaches of the Celtic West. In this respect they differ from so many of the volcanic coastal rocks of the Canaries, which to me often appear—and occasionally are—covered by a thin film of dried urine. Nor are all these rocks merely decorative. For a long line of them, three hundred yards out, forms a reef which breaks the force of the Atlantic

---

[1] The distinction between summer and winter seems at first ridiculous when only ten degrees Fahrenheit separate the warmest months from the coldest, and when the 'winter' offers so much more dependable sunshine than our own summer. But for the *canario* it is a reality. He is not being funny when he speaks of 'a dry summer' or 'a cold winter'. The fisherman at San Felipe on the north coast of Gran Canaria who remarked one balmy December evening as we strolled together through the banana plantations, 'This is the time of year when we are all coughing and sneezing,' had a very genuine cold himself. The upper reaches of Las Palmas society, however, merit the charge of affectation when their womenfolk blossom forth each 'autumn' in new tweed costumes.

rollers, so that Las Canteras is not only golden, not only clean, but also calm.

The brown or browning bodies covering it are as likely as not to have blonde hair. For the tourist invasion of Las Palmas is above all a Viking invasion. A few scouts had already arrived in 1960, when a friendly Finn who had founded a fashion house here directed me to an excellent Swedish restaurant on the promenade. Now every barman and chambermaid has a few words of *Svensk*; and whole blocks of apartments have been bought by the big agencies of Stockholm and Copenhagen to shelter the tourists for whom hotel accommodation is insufficient and too expensive.

For these Scandinavian package tours are extraordinarily cheap. £35 can cover a two week holiday with bed, board, and 6,000 miles' flying included. Tasty meals are given in exchange for vouchers in dozens of *smörgåsbord* serving restaurants between Las Canteras and the port; and a holiday in Las Palmas evokes in the contemporary Scandinavian mind the same mixture of brash vulgarity, beer swilling, and fake Spanish atmosphere as a holiday in Majorca.

In Britain short holidays in Las Palmas are still designed for the luxury market. This is partly because charter flights there have neither been tailored down to the economy class nor aggressively promoted. But it is also partly because British links with Las Palmas are of long standing, and still bear the impression of a more leisured age, when travelling was for the rich.

So that to find the quarter of the city where the Englishman will feel most at home we must leave Las Canteras and the Parque Santa Catalina and travel over a mile south, past that other beach, Las Alcaravaneras. Because it adjoins the port it is less attractive, though anywhere else in the islands its golden sands would be a feature to be proud of. Soon after it ends begins the *Ciudad Jardín*, a garden suburb developed by an early and happy alliance of British and Spanish capital thirty or forty years before Hampstead and Welwyn. Here stands the English church. Here the British Club. Here the Club Náutico. And here, where many a retired Empire builder has prolonged his days, stands the Hotel Atlántico, the Victorian bastion in Las Palmas as is the Pension Spragg in

Gran Canaria

Santa Cruz de Tenerife. I swear that I saw an aspidistra in the hall.

A little way beyond these, exactly midway between port and old town, stands a green oasis which is at once many things. It is a public park, with zoo, swimming pool, and tennis courts. It contains a luxury hotel, the flagship of the great H.U.S.A.[1] chain: to see how truly luxurious a hotel still can be in this Hiltonian age one must visit the Santa Catalina if only for a coffee. And this oasis is also the tourist shop window of Gran Canaria.

El Pueblo Canario is its name, the Canary Village, with souvenir shops, 'typical' cafés, and frequent performances of local dancing. For those who are carried there willy-nilly from their cruise ship it may seem the embodiment of all that is worst in such artificial villages, with overtones of Anacapri, of *Swissminiatur*, or of Barcelona's *Pueblo Español*. Yet the handicrafts for sale are of high quality, the dancers have won prizes at international folklore festivals. Their lovely costumes were once the gala dress of ordinary peasant folk. And the strains to which they move, altogether happier and without the haunting melancholy of the Tenerife songs, belong to Gran Canaria alone.

Above all, the buildings themselves of the *Pueblo Canario* have a dramatic unity shared by few such complexes. For they are the conception of a single architect, or rather artist, a presiding genius to whom it is time we paid our homage.

His temple is set back a little on one side of the 'village' square. It is a museum with a difference: everything it contains is the work of the single man after whom it was named—Néstor de la Torre. It is a museum in which I find myself peculiarly at home. As I wander from room to room I slip deliciously deeper and deeper back into a childhood more than half forgotten. The colours of the canvases, the other-worldliness of the fantasies, the very textures

---

[1] Hoteles Unidos Sociedad Anonima. They are well entrenched in the Canaries, with the Metropol as well as the Santa Catalina itself in Las Palmas; with the Mencey in Santa Cruz de Tenerife; and with the Taoro in Puerto de la Cruz. The Mencey dates from only just before the Civil War, and has been largely extended since. Yet its beautiful woodwork, its vast leather armchairs, and its spacious halls are of a style and quality of craftsmanship which went out in British hotels before 1914.

of the furnishings plumb distant levels of my subconscious, bringing momentarily to the surface the drawing-room of a town house where in best suit and on best behaviour I was occasionally taken to tea, or the lily pond of a country garden where I spent one sunny afternoon when I was four.

Those much older or younger than myself are unlikely to fall so completely under Néstor's charm. For living from 1887 to 1938 he came under the influence of all those movements: Impressionism, Art Nouveau, and even Surrealism, which were reflected, albeit at many removes, in the illustrations to children's books between the wars, and so coloured my own early memories. But however blinding 'the light of common day' outside the Hotel Santa Catalina, those of any age who take the trouble to step inside the Museo Néstor will see in his pictures the Canaries transfigured by a 'visionary gleam' which raises, on mountain or headland, 'imperial palaces'[1] filled with gaily clothed *canarios* laughing at some 'vision splendid' beyond our sight. And pausing for a few moments before his great series the *Poema del Mar*, we again 'have sight of that immortal sea' where we can 'hear the mighty waters rolling evermore'.

Travelling on parallel to the sea we reach the main shopping district at the square called Parque San Telmo, where the long main street changes its name from León y Castillo to Triana. A block away on the seaward side is the principal market. Both purse and figure will benefit from an occasional mouth-watering meal made up of bananas from Arucas, oranges from the Angostura Valley, and tomatoes from Juan Grande.

Triana ends in a strange little metal bridge over the dried river bed of the Guiniguada. Crossing it, we find that the streets give up all attempt to follow any regular pattern. We are at last in Las Palmas proper, the city which grew up within the invaders' original camp.

During three-quarters of a century after Béthencourt's landing in Lanzarote his successors the Perazas, vassals of the kings of Castile, failed to complete the conquest of the islands. Then in

[1] One of these palaces of Néstor's dreams has been translated into reality in the *Parador* of La Cruz de Tejeda.

1477 Diego de Herrera, who had married Inés Peraza, surrendered to the crown these rights to Gran Canaria, Tenerife and La Palma in return for a cash payment, and for certain privileges. These included his appointment as Count of La Gomera, an ominous title which here made its first appearance in Canary history.

Queen Isabella of Castile, thus free to act directly, lost no time in sending six hundred men accompanied by thirty nobles under the command of Juan Rejón, who landed in Gran Canaria on 24th June 1478. Almost five years later the last resistance ended, after a prolonged struggle in which the Spanish camp, protected by its stockade of palms (*palmas*), was three times besieged by the natives, whose two kings or *guanartemes* held their courts well inland, at Telde and at Galdar. Las Palmas inevitably became the new capital, as it had already become the ecclesiastical capital when a bull of Pope Sixtus IV, dated 29th August 1482, transferred there from Lanzarote the see of the Bishop of Canaria.

It very soon became more important still. One reason why the Crown had taken the conquest into its own hands was through fear that unless the Canaries were soon subdued they would fall to the Portuguese, already established in Madeira and in Cabo Verde, leaving the Spaniards with no base opposite the African coast, which was then the area offering most scope for imperial expansion.[1] By the Treaty of Alcaçobas-Toledo of 1480 Isabella finally secured from the Portuguese their promise not to interfere in the Canaries, leaving them in return the rest of the Atlantic.

The Catholic Queen thus unwittingly made sure of the New World. For not only was Isabella the only ruler prepared to back Columbus, but perhaps also the only one under whom he could have achieved success. Had he sailed due west from any European port his men might well have forced him to turn back before he had sighted the Indies. But he sailed instead from her own furthest west possessions, the Canaries, from which both winds and the

---

[1] For some thirty years in the late fifteenth century a Spanish bridgehead was fortified at Santa Cruz de la Mar Pequeña in the present day Rio de Oro. But four centuries were to pass before permanent occupation of this southern coast of 'Barbary'. For a fascinating travelogue on the Rio de Oro read *The Forbidden Coast* by John Lodwick.

Gran Canaria

'Canaries current' carried him towards the Caribbean, the same winds and current which in later centuries were to carry the infamous slavers over the terrible 'middle passage'.

Las Palmas, with its excellent port, at once became the staging post of literally 'crucial' importance on the way to the new lands. It is significant that Madrid never at any time interfered with direct trade between the Canaries and America, although all American trade with Spain itself was channelled through Seville alone. For the islands were in reality the first of Castile's overseas conquests. Las Palmas must have been a brash shanty town when only nine years after the last natives had laid down their arms Columbus sailed from here to Gomera and on over the ocean blue.

So that this old quarter, known as Vegueta, has at once similarities to Spanish colonial towns beyond the Atlantic, and connections with Columbus.

As in the older parts of the older cities of the New World, one has that indefinable sense of an old world atmosphere in which something is lacking. And that something is of course the Middle Ages. The Cathedral of Santa Ana, for example, a heavy stone building started in 1497 and restored and extended about 1800, pierces us with nostalgia for countless similar buildings across Europe which shelter at least the memory of some earlier, humbler temple. Its treasures, too; a pyx attributed to Benvenuto Cellini, the portrait of a bishop supposedly by Goya, and plate from old St. Paul's Cathedral, London, sold off during the Commonwealth, are treasures of that uncertain or secondhand kind characteristic of remote and newly settled provinces.

So, too, are many of the contents of the *Casa de Colón*, a museum installed in the early governor's residence: second-rate works by minor masters from the Prado's cellars, and furniture hardly fit for even a lesser stately home in England. But Columbus (*Colón*) did almost certainly stay here on his first, second, and fourth voyages of exploration, and the ground floor contains a fascinating collection of documents connected with him, religious paintings and statues which were already in the islands at the time of his visits, and contemporary charts and maps.

The well in the patio may be the only part of the building which stands just as he saw it; and likewise the *ermita* of San Antonio Abad nearby is merely a late eighteenth-century reconstruction on the site of the chapel where he heard Mass. But the *Casa de Colón*, and several other old houses in Vegueta, are interesting in themselves, as early stages in the architectural evolution which links Seville with Lima. Here the patio is still dominant, and the craftsmanship which later in Telde and Tenerife went into the balconies is in the *Casa de Colón* to be seen in the fine carved ceilings. For in their buildings as in their speech and their folklore the Canaries stand midway between Old World and New.

One corner of the Barrio de Vegueta requires no comparisons or connections to arouse our interest. This is the *Museo Canario*, with an excellent library (open only from 5 to 8 p.m.), a 'general collection' which is best avoided, and on the first floor the most extensive collection of prehistoric remains in the Canaries. Although neither so selective nor so well-arranged as that of the *Museo Archeológico* in Tenerife, there is more of it: case upon case of ceramics, and of the curious seal-like *pintaderas*, dozens of native mummies, and hundreds of their skulls. Examples of the skulls of several other races are thoughtfully provided to enable the amateur ethnologist to compare them and draw his own conclusions. One small room has maps in relief of all seven of the islands. Studying them the visitor soon learns why all roads in the Canaries are difficult, and which are the most difficult routes of all.

The first road which we shall take out of town is in fact an exception to this rule. If we arrived by air we shall already be familiar with it, for it is the main road south, which passes the airport of Gando. For the first five miles it is squeezed close against the sea by the same mountain formation which has forced ribbon development upon Las Palmas itself. Then, as the country opens out, a branch to the right allows us to follow a parallel course on higher ground, with better views.

It soon brings us to Telde, the second town of the island with over 40,000 inhabitants, and several apparent centres. Two should be visited. The first, the tree-shaded *plaza* by the church of San Juan, is on the main road, and is surrounded on two sides by houses with wooden balconies. The fifteenth-century church has an equally ancient carved Flemish reredos, and a curious life-size statue of Christ in corn-cob paste weighing only fifteen pounds.

The second, the quarter of San Francisco, still has the quiet atmosphere of the Canaries of seventy years ago, but is harder to find. Indeed, the short Canary sunset was over when, at the end of a cobbled street of white houses, I emerged in a silent square by the church, while behind the palms which stood above the high, white wall of the convent it once served, rose the moon.

Three miles beyond Telde a prominent hill to the left of the road is marked high up by four square indentations after which it is called Cuatro Puertas (Four Doors). Leaving the branch road to the airport on one's left, it is best to park one's transport where a sign on the main road points to Cuatro Puertas, and to proceed on foot.

The four doors, of regular shape and roughly equal size, are divided by no more than pillars, for behind them runs a large cave. It is quite certainly the work of primitive man, and it has been suggested that it was the home of vestal virgins, the seat of the *faicán* or High Priest, or a mortuary where the dead were embalmed. But these remain mere suggestions, and equally mysterious is the use given to other smaller, less regularly fashioned caves, just beyond the brow of the hill, and to a small flat terrace between them, in which has been cut a series of shallow channels.

Another important and equally baffling prehistoric remain lies in this part of the island, beside the Barranco de Balos beyond the villages of Ingenio and Agüimes. It is the hieroglyphic inscription described in Chapter I, which seems to belong to some form of alphabet.

Inland from Agüimes the road starts to climb, passing Santa Lucía and eventually San Bartolomé, from which it winds round into the Cumbre, the island's central massif, by a devious back-door route. Both villages bear the suffix 'de Tirajana,' the ancient and mysterious sounding name for all this district. And under the spell, perhaps, of Tirajana, Don Vicente Araña of Santa Lucía has gathered in his curious turretted residence there a remarkable amateur collection of native remains. If he is not at home himself his servant will gladly show you round El Castillo de la Fortaleza, as his house is called.

The mountains of Tirajana, however, are not typical of the landscape of southern Gran Canaria. For this we must bear left at Agüimes, returning to the main road from Las Palmas. If we drive straight across it we shall reach the tiny port of Arinaga, a summer retreat from the city, where practically every house is shut up in the 'winter'. But let us turn right, and speed on south, across one of the few coastal plains in the archipelago.

Obscure scientific jargon leaps to life when we suddenly face the phenomenon it describes. Thus 'micro-climate' has a tangible meaning for me since I have experienced the enormous variation in weather in different parts of one island. In all but the two eastern-most islands there is a contrast between a totally dry south and a not-quite-so-dry north, and Tenerife owes to its peak the bunching of every climate from semi-tropical to alpine within a distance— as the crow flies—of as little as ten miles.

Gran Canaria, although it can offer nothing above the snowline, is climatically as well as geographically a continent in miniature, and contains as many as six micro-climates. The weather maps of the island in Las Palmas newspapers are more complicated and exciting than those of Britain on our own television. While we are being offered 'Continuous drizzle from northern Scotland to the Humber: drizzle relieved by patches of fog in southern England,' the citizen of Las Palmas has the choice of cloud or sunshine, wind or calm, 50° or 80°, depending on whether he makes for the north, the south, the west, or the Cumbre.

Because the road south is so good, and the journey therefore so easy, it is here that the contrasts between micro-climates strike most forcibly. When Las Canteras is covered by cloud, or the Parque Santa Catalina is swept by light rain (it does happen!), the tourist soon learns to ask for a packet lunch and to take coach or taxi to Maspalomas. Before he has reached the tomato fields of Juan Grande he will be bowling along in brilliant sunshine.

It is a sunshine which today spells security for the inhabitants and wealth for the landowner, who bears the mellifluent title of Conde de la Vega Grande. The villages on his estates can be recognized by their rows of new concrete cubes, the houses of his labour force. They sound awful but in fact are not unpleasing, their monotony being broken by clever decorative use of the perforated concrete walls which more usually serve as windbreaks protecting banana plantations.

Criticism of feudalism should be tempered by reflection that new houses are only necessary because the Count first laid the pipes to bring the transforming water. I was told that it was an Englishman who first grew tomatoes here less than twenty years ago, and the agricultural revolution he set in train has required an influx of workers into an area which a generation ago subsisted miserably by the export of its labour.

Nor are the Count's entrepreneurial talents restricted to the land. While one of his two sons manages the farms, the other directs the development of the coast, through a holding company which may succeed in giving its well-chosen name to this entire southern seaboard: Costa Canaria S.A.

When first I knew Spain its only 'Costa' was the well-established Costa Brava. Now 'Costa' This and 'Costa' That multiply till they rival in number the 'Côtes' of France. But I shall not complain if Costa Canaria is added to Costa Blanca, Costa Dorada and the rest, because it may displace the loose use of the name Maspalomas.

Maspalomas itself is a village about two miles from the sea, belonging to the Conde de la Vega Grande. A promontory stretching south into the ocean has naturally been called the Punta (Point) of Maspalomas. Currents and tidal forces have built up to the west of this promontory a golden beach backed by the biggest sand dunes in the Canaries. This is the Playa de Maspalomas, near which stands the lighthouse which marks the promontory, the Faro de Maspalomas. And running inland is a tidal lagoon called the Charco de Maspalomas. The name applies to nothing outside this relatively small area.

The oasis-like combination of palms, lagoon, and sand-dunes beside the ocean is exotic, and has attracted a unique flora and fauna. Vast numbers of migrating birds, in particular, call here: *más palomas* simply means 'more pigeons'. But the human species is now disturbing their habitat. I found roads being driven through the palm grove in readiness for chalets and a hotel.

As yet, however, there was not even the smallest pension, and by five o'clock in the afternoon, when the last hired car had driven off back to Las Palmas, I had the whole gigantic film set—it has been used for several films—to myself. The only living beings for several miles were busy at work: the lighthouse keepers, and the Americans at the nearby Mercury tracking station who contact and report to Cape Kennedy on the progress of spacecraft.

After sunset it became distinctly eerie, and I used to drive back to the village of Maspalomas to revive my spirits on *caña*, the common man's drink in Gran Canaria. It is white rum, made from the sugar cane which for the first century after the conquest was the island's principal crop.

From conversations with the people of the village I learnt what life was like before tomatoes and the Costa Canaria: of the years when no rain meant no food, and when the only never-failing water supply was a single small spring near the sea.[1] They are hardly affluent even today, these gentle soft-voiced men in cotton shirts and trousers and wide-brimmed straw hats, with a little over £2.50 a week each (in 1966). But they told me that their houses were provided free, and with pride rather than resentment they showed me the farm, the bakery, and the big house where the Count or members of his family spend only a few days each year.

'It is a little *amargo* (bitter)' said one, however, 'when prices go up so much quicker than our wages. Of course it is due to the tourists and the Costa Canaria.'

The first part of the Costa Canaria to be developed was the beach of San Agustín, on the main road four miles before Maspalomas. The chalets are expensive, well-built, and beautifully situated. The restaurant and shops serving them are simply expensive. The basic menu at the restaurant costs 40 per cent of the weekly wage of a labourer such as I had spoken to. Tins of food at the grocery cost twice as much as in Las Palmas supermarkets. And in the newspaper shop I looked in vain for the *Diario de Las Palmas* amongst the dailies of Helsinki, Hamburg, Stockholm, Amsterdam and Lon-

[1] See footnote Chapter Two, Lanzarote, page 46.

don. The shopgirl positively turned her nose up when I asked for it:
'We sell no Spanish papers here.'

Although I have no sympathy with such an attitude, and feel
deeply ill at ease in such an artificial imported atmosphere, I must
admit that even the most modest and carefully inoffensive developments in the poorer parts of the Canaries are bound to make a
violent break with local life.

At the other end of the Costa Canaria, for example, ten miles
beyond Maspalomas, lies the fishing village of Arguineguín. It
will inevitably attract development, for behind it runs a delightful
green *barranco*; and only a mile beyond is the small but sheltered
beach of Pata la Vaca, protected by cliffs from the strong winds
which afflict every southern coast in the islands, and from which
the Playa de Maspalomas itself is not exempt. But there will be no
possibility of adapting any buildings of the existing village, and
they are so primitive in construction that whatever is built new
cannot avoid clashing with them.[1] I feel no more at ease amidst the
huts of Arguineguín, or the hovels of Gran Tarajal in Fuerteventura, than I do amidst the sickly sophistication of San Agustín,
although for opposite reasons.

Perhaps there is an inevitable initial discord in the marriage
between the children of the sun and the children of the north.
Torremolinos is no less ghastly than Puerto de la Cruz. We must
remember that the urbane delights of the Côte d'Azur have had a
long century to mature since Lord Brougham and his followers
first raped the Provençal coast.

In theory it is possible to drive beyond Arguineguín; at first near
the sea, then inland through Mogán and over a tortuous route
through tangled country to the most isolated village of Gran
Canaria, San Nicolás. Its isolation has permitted the survival there
—and there alone—of a species of partridge, *Alectorix rufa*, locally
known as *la Perdiz de la Aldea*. For San Nicolás is often known
simply as *la Aldea*, perhaps because until recently it was the
only village that the peasants of this far west ever knew. It stands
in a profound *barranco* which runs inland all the way up to Tejeda,
thus allowing those wonderful views from the *Parador* terrace.

[1] In 1971 the fisher-folk of Arguineguín were being re-housed in
completely new streets of 'council houses'.

Gran Canaria

After this one great break in the coastline, the mountains crowd together to make an even more formidable obstacle for the thirty miles of road which run high above the sea to link San Nicolás to Agaete, and so to Las Palmas. Drivers are aware of the dangers, and no accident has yet occurred at the worst point of all, the dizzy drop of Andén Verde. But I have never dared to drive along this road myself, and instead approached *la Aldea* by *guagua*. My most direct knowledge of this region is therefore from sorties I made down from the Cumbre.

Even this limited exploration was enough to convince me that the far west of Gran Canaria is, with the far north of La Palma, the least known and the most rewarding region in the Canaries.

All the guide books traditionally describe the interior of Gran Canaria under the three routes, southern, central and northern, which correspond at once to the three main roads out of Las Palmas, and to the excursions offered by the travel agencies. The system is logical because the physical structure of the island only allows a few, often narrow, cross-country roads linking these three main routes; and because even with their own transport, most visitors are forced to return to Las Palmas at the end of each day's drive through lack of suitable accommodation anywhere else. A four-day off-the-main-road itinerary which I followed myself when showing the island to my family made use of the Guayarmina hotel at Berrazales spa for the first night, and the Cruz de Tejeda *Parador* for the second. But then we had to camp out at Maspalomas for the third!

Having now covered the traditional southern route, I feel bound to continue with the central route, which leaves Las Palmas from the square in front of the cathedral. (There is no possibility of reaching it by any short cut from the port or from Las Canteras.) And having embarked on this, I must at once admit that in this particular part of the countryside there are several excellent hotels, including two which are English owned and managed: the Lentiscal at Tafira Alta and the famous Santa Brigida, which is at Monte Coello and not at Santa Brigida itself.

But this whole district, although high above the city in beautiful surroundings, is for practical purposes a series of residential suburbs, linked to Las Palmas by frequent *guaguas* and *piratas*.[1] Although known generically as 'El Monte', they in fact progress over five miles, through Tafira Baja and Tafira Alta—already at 1,230 feet—to Monte Coello and to Santa Brigida at 1,600 feet.

Anyone staying there would find enough to visit day by day on foot for at least a week without leaving the immediate district. Its attractions have long been recognized, as is proved by the many mellow old houses with their well matured gardens. Indeed the whole area is like a garden; for here, as so rarely happens in the Canaries, no one crop dominates. Instead, in a happy blend of temperate and tropical, we find apples, pears, bananas, oranges, lemons and vines.

From the vines comes the best red wine in the islands: *vino del Monte*. The viticulturist of Tacoronte in Tenerife would disagree, but I have tasted both. It is dry yet full-bodied, with the consistency of a madeira and the bouquet of a burgundy. Although only produced in relatively small quantities, and therefore not available retail, a few enquiries from the country folk will lead to the unlocking of a small stone *bodega*, and the filling of an empty bottle or two at about 25 pesetas each.

Appropriately situated at the heart of this garden of the Canaries is the publicly owned *Jardín Canario*. Here are gathered all forms of plant life found in the archipelago—in contrast to the *Jardín Botanico* of Orotava which seeks to acclimatize plants from other parts of the world. It stands above the lovely Angostura Valley (which has no connection with Angostura bitters, except that Angostura, now Ciudad Bolivar, in Venezuela, which gave its name to them, was presumably founded by *canarios*). This can be explored by a road which runs along the valley parallel to the main road high above.

[1] A wonderful word, used above all in Gran Canaria to describe taxis and micro-buses which, by filling every available seat, can afford to charge no more on the country routes than the regular *guaguas*. Running directly without intermediate stops, they are quicker as well as more comfortable. Once they may have been unofficial, and pirates in the eyes of the regular services; but they are quite within the law today. The visitor will run no risk and save time by travelling '*en pirata*'.

There is just as much to see on the other, southern side of the main road. From Monte Coello a good road has been built in cork-screw fashion to the highest point of what is nothing other than the side of a volcano, which falls steeply on the other side into a perfectly formed crater, the Caldera de Bandama. It is long extinct, and a small farm has been carved out of the bottom. This farm has now, unfortunately, been purchased for development, so that it will soon be as spoiled as the peak from which we look down, with its souvenir shop and its expensive café.

Two miles beyond the turning for Bandama another road, lead-ing eventually to Telde, takes one to La Atalaya, known for its pottery and for its cave dwellings. I merely record this, for the pottery of Chipude in Gomera is more genuinely primitive, and the cave dwellings of Artenara which we shall be visiting later in this chapter, are more impressively situated. But not all of us have the time to visit these remote places, and those wishing to see the troglodytes of La Atalaya should leave the village of 'proper' houses on the main road and strike away to the right along the footpaths which wind round the hillsides from 'front door' to 'front door'. A little discreetly expressed interest and admiration will secure an invitation to enter one of the under-ground homes.

From Santa Brigida the road climbs rapidly through the chest-nut forests to San Mateo. In less than five miles we travel as far climatically as from Provence to Brittany. Another five miles takes us to Las Lagunetas, where we might be on the latitude of Connemara, or even Skye. Dark-eyed, red-cheeked people, the men often wearing the heavy woollen *manta* or cloak common in the Canary highlands, stare at us through the mist as they pause from lifting the potatoes. Like the Irish, they even have an emigration problem; for at certain seasons half the population will be at work in the south gathering the tomatoes of the Conde de la Vega Grande.

After another three miles a road branches off steeply to the left, to climb to the Cruz de Tejeda. The usual circular tour from Las Palmas consists in driving up to the *Parador* for lunch, dropping down again to this junction, and then instead of return-

12. Gran Canaria: life remains quiet in the interior, away from the great city. Note how corner-stones of lava-built church have been left unpainted for contrast

13. Gran Canaria: the mountain village of Tejeda (p. 103)

14. Tenerife: altar of the sanctuary of the Cristo de la Laguna (p. 117)

15. Tenerife: the strange world of Las Cañadas at over 7,000 feet (pp. 144–5)

16. Tenerife: landscape broken by crater

ing along the road we have travelled by El Monte, turning off north.

This takes us, after perhaps even more twists and turns, down to the sizeable town of Teror. Like Telde it has several streets of old houses, and although only a quarter the size it has one feature which Telde lacks: a definite centre, formed by the square around the huge church of Nuestra Señora del Pino. The present building dates from 1765, but there has been a church here ever since 1481, beside the pine tree (*pino*) in the branches of which there appeared in that year an image of the Virgin.

It was a convenient date for her appearance. The conquest was well under way, and the conversion and pacification of the natives was the main problem facing the invaders. Teror, too, was a convenient place for her to appear. It was deep in the interior yet within reach of Las Palmas. It was intermediate between the two native 'capitals' of Galdar and Telde. And it was on the edge of that Selva de Doramas, the forest which had been the favourite refuge of that noble leader, Doramas, whose death a few months earlier marked the beginning of the end of native resistance.

The growth of her cult was probably spontaneous enough, and the authorities certainly did nothing to prevent it. Her wardrobe filled with jewels and beautifully worked robes. Three convents were founded in the town (one of them, now a palace of the Bishops of Las Palmas, stands on a raised garden behind the church). When the original pine tree fell down, one grown from its seed was planted in its place.

Her feast day is 8th September; but it is early in December that she makes her great annual journey, being carried down to the capital to proceed slowly the whole length of the León y Castillo and Triana. She then rests for a week in the cathedral while her devotees file past. No less than one hundred and fifty thousand souls assisted at her progress the December that I was in Las Palmas. Watching and listening to them, I realized that her little figure had helped to unite the great city to its hinterland. If there seems little here of that struggle between country and town which divides so many islands—Tenerife not excepted—some of the credit must go to the *patrona* of all Gran Canaria, country and town alike.

Gran Canaria

To the north-west of Teror, by roads which advance one mile for every three they cover, lie Firgas and Moya. We are on the edge of what until the early nineteenth century was still primeval forest as Doramas knew it, and the countryside is increasingly luxuriant. At one point on the road between Firgas and Moya is something almost unknown in the Canaries: a damp patch where a rivulet drains away down a mossy bank. One spring at the head of a valley behind Firgas has medicinal properties, and is bottled commercially to serve as the 'tonic' accompanying the whiskies and brandies which are so extensively advertised and consumed in this happy, duty-free land.

Ten miles due north of Teror, and ten miles out of Las Palmas on what we have referred to as the northern route, lies Arucas. It has been called the banana capital of the Western hemisphere, but the Canaries could offer half a dozen contenders for such a title. It is, however, a pleasant, distinctive town, not much smaller than Telde, with a flower-lined approach road and a big black basalt church, and it is backed by a perfect conical hill, at first appearance too steep for any road to climb. In fact, however, a well-made highway winds round and round to the acre of level plateau at the summit.

Here, with views across the green sea of bananas from La Isleta to the Montaña de Galdar, interrupted by the frequent gleam of an irrigation tank, and across the sea itself from Lanzarote to Tenerife, stands an excellent new restaurant. Amongst other meals I have eaten a Christmas dinner here, and have only praise for its cooking, service, and charges. There is, unfortunately, no possibility of overnight accommodation.

From Arucas the road drops swiftly to run between banana plantations and the sea along the north coast. The name of the first village passed through, Bañaderos, may tempt us to swim. But the rollers break fiercely, while an undertow sucks away. Local advice should be followed as to the safest of the little black beaches. The most curious of the villages is El Roque, a cubist fantasy atop a single sea-surrounded rock.

Soon after, an abrupt cliff allows no room beside the sea, and the road begins to climb the steep Cuesta de Silva. A signpost to the left shows the footpath to the Cenobio (monastery) de Valerón, a seven-storeyed labryinth of caves of great importance before the conquest, but, like Cuatro Puertas, of quite uncertain use. Safer parking while visiting the caves can be found on the level stretch of road at the summit, from which there are fine views.

Whatever the purpose of the Cenobio de Valerón, it was situated in the natives' heartland. For the landscape before us is dominated by the ugly Montaña de Galdar, the only hill I have ever mistaken for a slag heap. And Galdar itself was always one of their two capitals, and for a time sole capital of the island. Pedro de Vera, who succeeded Juan Rejón as commander of the invaders, realized its importance, and established a garrison at Agaete under Alonso de Lugo (note this name) to attack it from the rear. His strategy was soon proved correct. First the noble Doramas of Telde was mortally wounded in a skirmish. Then the king, or *guanarteme* of Galdar himself, Artemi Semidán, was captured and sent to Spain. Galdar fell, and resistance drew away to the centre of the island.

It is a pleasant town, with one of Gran Canaria's few dragon trees visible behind the grille of the *ayuntamiento* patio. The dark church is supposed to stand near the site of the *guanarteme*'s cave-palace, and its font was used for the baptism of many of the conquered natives.

Not for the baptism of Artemi Semidán himself, however. That took place at Calatayud in distant Aragon, once the home of the poet Martial, and a town stranger in atmosphere to my mind than Galdar will ever be. His godparents were the Catholic sovereigns themselves, and he took his godfather's name to become Don Fernando Guanarteme. After a year he was allowed to return to Gran Canaria, where, convinced by now of the overwhelming superiority of the Europeans, he tried without great success to persuade those still resisting to surrender.

He settled down peacefully enough himself under the new order, and in due course led contingents of *canarios* to assist in the invasions of La Palma and later of Tenerife. This was not 'unpatriotic', for the natives in the various islands, being without ships, knew nothing of one another. His own defeat had been brought about by a force which included natives from Gomera, who provided his enemies with a primitive form of radio communication by their whistling language.[1]

At the north-western point of the island lies the small port of Sardina, sometimes called Sardina del Norte to distinguish it from a less important Sardina in the tomato lands of the south. It may have a future as a resort: the swimming, certainly, is better than on the rapidly developing resorts of Tenerife's north coast. But then I was in a mood to share in the vision of the dynamic contractor who, like a Heroic Age chieftain, summoned us into the hall of the block of flats which were rising above him.

I was with the Danish friends to whom I owe many photographs in this book, and tingling from our Boxing Day swim we sat down with his workmen to a typically Canarian menu of fish, those delicious salt-cooked potatoes called *papas arrugadas*, and rum. As we ate, our host, a fine, large-boned man of obviously indigenous ancestry, with the Guanche-sounding name of Tacoronte, expounded the touristic potentialities of Sardina. And all the while through the unglazed windows came a stream of Italian opera from the mouth of a swimmer who only ceased when he plunged underwater, to recommence his *aria* immediately he surfaced. He, too, was evidently satisfied with Sardina.

Thirty years ago, before good roads had been built, Sardina and Puerto de las Nieves, the next little port down the coast, were regular ports of call for the mail steamers, and must both have been equally remote. Now Sardina is the less visited, for the road 'dies' there, whereas the road to Puerto de las Nieves is part of the circular route round the island. Standing at night on the shingle beach of this last village, or at the end of the jetty, one sees every now and again what appear to be twin comets high up away to the left, now describing some irregular parabola, and now again lost to view. They are the headlights of some car or lorry, feeling its way along the narrow *corniche* from San Nicolás, a thousand feet or more above the sea.

[1] They were led by the Conde de la Gomera, Hernán Peraza, and stationed at Agaete under Alonso de Lugo, who was in later years to marry Peraza's widow, Beatriz de Bobadilla.

Gran Canaria

Many of the clients of the two fish restaurants in Puerto de las Nieves are from no further afield than Agaete, less than a mile's stroll up the road, and the natural capital of the valley which bears its name. We have seen how Alonso de Lugo was landed here to unlock the back door of the *guanarteme* of Galdar; and after the conquest he was granted the valley and settled down here, planting sugar cane and building one of the first sugar refineries on the island. Most of us would have been content to end our days in this realm of gold amid the western islands, but Alonso Fernández de Lugo was a contemporary of stout Cortés, and required no peaks in Darien to stimulate his wild surmises. Whenever he looked down the valley out to sea, unsubdued Tenerife rose before him.

The valley will produce not only sugar cane, but almost everything imaginable. Here grow as many fruits as in the Angostura valley. Here almond trees blossom uncannily in midwinter. Here every white cottage is surrounded by flowers, and the road itself is lined with hibiscus and poinsettia.[1]

Right at the valley's head stands one of the best hotels in the Canaries. Yet because the Hotel Guayarmina (named after a native princess) was originally built for visitors to the Berrazales spa a few yards down the hill, it only fills up during the summer, when the people of Las Palmas come out to take the waters. In winter I have had the shady gardens and the comfortable lounges almost to myself, with the choice of the dozens of armchairs scattered over the three vast balconies. Three times a week a coach load or two on the excursion from Las Palmas bring a little life from the outside world. But as they return down the valley peace flows back from the pine forest of Tamadaba, 4,000 feet above, and one is left with two or three congenial fellow residents, long term winterers such as Mr. Nuttall, Kristina Lafquist, or Madame Neuve.

It is in Tamadaba that I wish to end our visit to Gran Canaria, and to reach it I propose to take you on the day's journey which I made there myself.

I started from the far south, from an outlying estate of the Conde de la Vega Grande near Maspalomas. When I had gone to his

[1] Though the flowers of the valley of Agaete remain the loveliest in Gran Canaria, they had been sadly reduced in 1971 by the tapping of the springs to supply the needs of Arucas and Las Palmas.

administrator's house to ask permission to park there for the night, I was invited to stay for a talk, and prevailed upon to sit down. But his womenfolk continued to stand respectfully around us, as we talked in the warm January air, gazing from the terrace as the sun swiftly set over the Costa Canaria.

I was up before it had risen again, and breakfasted some miles on and a thousand feet higher, where the road gives one last magnificent view south to the already distant lighthouse, before twisting down and around. For a long way there is no cultivation and seemingly no possibility of cultivation. Then at a widening of the *barranco* appears an oasis of vegetation, and a cluster of sloping tiled roofs.

It is these roofs which impress all the other inhabitants of Gran Canaria, and it is certainly odd that they should be found in one of its dryest corners, when on the north coast most buildings have a flat roof serving as terrace, or *azotea*. But the roofs are only a part of the charm of Fataga, this remote little village which might serve as the background to a southern version of our own fairy tales, purged of the lingering gloom of our Teutonic past.

Little cobbled paths run between the tiny one-storeyed cottages. Geraniums and bougainvillaea splash against their white walls. Oranges grow in their gardens. Although poor, their friendly owners are freeholders; and I learnt that for £150 I could join their number, acquiring thus a two-roomed cottage with a fine prospect, an outside oven, and a couple of acres of *barranco* on which to plant almond trees. And Maspalomas only ten miles away!

When I said that I was on my way to Tamadaba, the village baker told me that his cousin was the forest guard there, and wrote his name on a piece of paper. So pocketing this introduction I drove off again, climbing up and up into the hill country of Tirajana, of which the capital is the gloomy withdrawn village of San Bartolomé, still the 'town hall' for Maspalomas and the entire Costa Canaria.

Here I turned left, and after another climb passed through a cutting which no map marks, but which is as decisive a break as the pass between Lagunetas and the Cruz de Tejeda. Before me lay all the unknown west of Gran Canaria, and the dirt road which I followed for the next twenty miles, clinging high to the shoulder of the Cumbre, at every turn gave tantalizing hints of its treasures. Here a scattering of Canary pines. There a denser gathering of them against a skyline. Then came a sudden glitter far below.

Twice before when passing that way I had resisted the siren-like fascination of the Cercado reservoir.[1] Today, however, I yielded to the temptress and took a track to the left, dropping rapidly below pine level and past two or three remote—and how remote! —farmsteads, to eat my lunch beside this enchanted artificial lake in a land of few men and less water.

On returning to the main road I passed a single tiny hamlet, its main crop evidently the almonds which lay in piles by the roadside, and then entered the wildest part of the Cumbre. The summit, at the Pozo de las Nieves, was out of view to the right, but the road wound round the base of a mountain crowned by the 350-foot monolith called the Roque Nublo. Soon after, on the other side at a lower level, stood a thicker rock resembling a fortress.

And a fortress Bentaiga was for the last native defenders after the fall of Galdar, and even after Fernando Guanarteme, returning from Spain, persuaded his uncle the *faicán* or High Priest of Galdar to surrender Fataga. They still retained enough morale to snatch a last victory from the invaders at Ajódar; but the former king again urged peace, and this time with success.

The most prominent amongst the pacified natives who entered Las Palmas on 24th April 1483 were the royal princesses of Galdar, whose surrender marked the end of resistance more finally than the capture of the king had done. This circumstance, coupled with all the caves vaguely associated with vestal virgins, has led to the hypothesis—it can be no more—that the pre-conquest society of Gran Canaria was matriarchal.

Beyond Tejeda village the road climbs 1,500 feet to the stone cross, the Cruz de Tejeda, beside which stands the *Parador* of

---

[1] An even larger reservoir, invisible from the road, is that of La Cueva de las Niñas. It is called after yet another supposed convent of vestal virgins (*niñas* means girls) of pre-conquest times. The water conservation policy of this very dry and very populous island has been particularly well carried out.

Néstor's dreams. If not a place where dreams become reality, it is certainly a spot where solid objects acquire a dream-like insubstantiality. From the terrace one follows the tangled pattern from Roque Nublo to Bentaiga and down the profound Barranco de San Nicolás: then across a sea of clouds to what appears to be the distant culmination of the same mountain system. Or can it be some cloud mirage? It is Teide.

Leaving to my right the routes back to Las Palmas, I drove on west, along a road clinging precariously to an almost forty-five degrees slope of what looked like coal dust. This had once been the inner edge of a great crater, and in this unlikely soil hundreds of small Canary pines were struggling for life: one of many praiseworthy efforts to restore to the islands their legacy of forest.

Although no longer quite as high as at La Cruz de Tejeda, I was still travelling at over 4,000 feet when a village came into view. It was Artenara, which not surprisingly is the highest village in Gran Canaria. The few houses around the parish church by the roadside are less than the eighth of the iceberg. Ask for la Virgen de la Cuevita, and you will be directed up a narrow footpath which in a few yards takes you to a hillside from which Roque Nublo and Bentaiga are again in full view. The entire hillside is like a gigantic rabbit warren, and every few yards stands the door of a house excavated in the easily worked *toba* rock.

After a few hundred yards a small terrace has been regularly paved outside the most important of these caves, which is a church, complete with altar, pulpit, and confessional, alike carved out of the same stone. It measures about twenty-five feet across, and is about fourteen feet high. Its much venerated image is no doubt older than her sanctuary, which in its present form probably dates from the seventeenth century, being built perhaps on the initiative of the friars of the Franciscan convent of San Antonio of Galdar, who for long provided this remote locality with spiritual care.

They had every reason to establish some attractive cult here, to wean the natives away from their memories of a past of which they were ever reminded by the rock of Bentaiga facing them across the valley. Documents tell us that half a century after the conquest the inhabitants were still completely pagan. My own guess is that the people of Artenara, with those of Chipude in Gomera, preserve a higher proportion of native blood in their veins than any others in the archipelago.

Their persistence in dwelling in caves would then be merely a continuation of their forbears' tradition. They do not yet see large numbers of tourists, and will gladly show you their clean, comfortable homes, which, as they say, are cool in summer and warm in winter.

The road continued on and up. I passed an occasional pine tree. Presently they came in twos and threes. Then they became so numerous that the magnificent panorama on both sides was lost to view. I was in the forest of Tamadaba.

Once all the archipelago above the 1,000-foot level was like this, before the farmer and the goat set to work—and much forest had probably gone even before the Spaniards landed. After a couple of miles I came upon two half-timbered houses all by themselves in a clearing. It was already evening, and the temperature and the place alike might have belonged to Scotland or to Scandinavia. Even the rough but friendly figure who came towards me in the gathering gloom had the apple cheeks of a countryman of one of England's cider counties. From his cap and badge I could tell that he was a forest guard.

After inviting me to spend the night beside his house he enquired my nationality, age, occupation, and finally what route I had followed to reach there.

'Fataga? You came through Fataga? Why, I'm from Fataga myself.'

'Of course you are,' I cried, causing him even more astonishment. 'I was talking to your cousin, only this morning.'

'Claudio Cazorla Reyes? Yes, indeed, this is his handwriting,' he said, taking the piece of paper from me. 'Welcome to Tamadaba!'

It was dead silent when I opened the door of my van after dinner, but fortunately the moon was up, although by no means full. Almost directly beneath me to the right, I knew, lay the spa of Berrazales. But I made my way to the left, until I could see the lights of Agaete, and other tiny lights far beyond. These were fishing boats in the channel between Gran Canaria and Tenerife, almost 5,000 feet below.

I stood there, reserving for daylight the more detailed exploration of the line where the forest abruptly ends, and of the region which still bears the name of Tirma. For my little pilgrimage was in order to honour and not to emulate the two last defenders of native freedom: Bentejuí and the *faicán* of Telde. From a high rock somewhere hereabouts they threw themselves into the abyss with a cry of defiance which has run down the centuries long after the language to which it belonged has perished.

'*Atis Tirma.*'

The most evident change in five years' absence from Gran Canaria has been the deterioration in the quality of life in Las Palmas itself. Pollution of the environment stands out more harshly in a sub-tropical than in a temperate climate, just as the hideous blocks of cheap flats on the newly-developed heights stand out more starkly against the brighter sky. Traffic becomes ever denser, despite the construction of an alternative route along the seafront on reclaimed land, and of a motorway to the north coast which avoids the steep, narrow wind through Arucas.

With the occupation of the Parque Santa Catalina by crowds of the smoothest-looking operators I ever wish to see, the hippies have gone west. The Cueva de las Niñas has in recent winters sheltered very different communities from that of the Vestal Virgins of before the Conquest.

The Costa Canaria, though still one vast building site, is beginning to mellow. The raw walls of the new apartments are already concealed by bougainvillea. An 'Ecumenical Temple' of enterprising design was opened by a Cardinal in 1971 at Playa del Inglés, to serve as a place of worship for every denomination, as well as for lectures and concerts.

The dunes of Maspalomas have meanwhile become a vast unofficial nudist colony, the resort at once of teenage Swedes and of septuagenarian Germans.

Yet the few hotels in the interior remain half empty. Santa Brigida, or the blessed Guayarmina at the head of the valley of Agaete, remain havens in a hectic island.

5

Tenerife

In the last chapter I compared Tenerife unfavourably with the other principal island. Now in imagination I stand on deck facing the hanging suburbs of Santa Cruz, a vertical city by comparison with the horizontal Las Palmas. The jagged chain of Anaga stretches away to my right. If we are still sufficiently far out at sea a tiny white triangle, the peak of Teide, peeps above the intervening heights behind La Laguna and Güimar. And I am filled with remorse, with tenderness and warmth towards an old love that I have betrayed. Every turn of that coastline, every square of that city, and many a contour of those sharply angled mountains could tell of happy moments that we have shared together.

Shared? No: the giving was always on her side, while I selfishly seized the pleasure so freely offered. Why then does she now smile at me as when first we met, as if my betrayal had never been? If in reality I were to land again I know that there would be no re-criminations, but instead the same bright and sunny welcome as before. Such forgiveness is surely unparalleled in a lover.

But then I am in the presence of something more than a lover. For did not the natives of all the islands alike worship Teide as a god?

It is time that we sampled this welcome, whether vicariously from our armchairs, or because we are numbered amongst the lucky ones, and have come south.

There is no division here between port and city. Ships berth right in the centre of Santa Cruz. Even if we do not step into one of the cheap and modern taxis, a few minutes' walk will take us into the Plaza de España, of which two sides are bordered by the sea, and one by the General Post Office and the Cabildo Insular (which contains the excellent Archaeological Museum).

The tall column in the centre of the square commemorates those who fell in the Civil War, and is a landmark we shall already have seen out at sea. On the fourth side, where begins the wide rectangular street called the Plaza de Candelaria, stands a more curious monument, in which the Italian sculptor Canova has represented the Virgin of Candelaria surrounded by four Guanche kings. It is a period piece of 1778 when the Spanish court, under the half Italian Charles III who had served his royal apprenticeship as King of Naples, still thought internationally, and when the *canarios* had never questioned the benefits of Spanish conquest. For these four 'loyal' kings are those of Güimar, Abona, Icod and Daute, who, because they offered no resistance to Alonso de Lugo, appeal least to all who now take pride in their *fuerte sangre indigena*.

These cautious rulers stand just in front of the principal resort of modern Tinerfeño society, the sumptuously appointed Casino. Foreigners may obtain temporary membership of this club, and even without this formality can ask to be taken upstairs to see Canary-inspired murals by Néstor de la Torre and José Aguiar.

Few visitors in fact need to join the Casino, for a ready-made club with no membership fees stands just round the corner, facing the Plaza de España. Sitting on the terrace of the Atlántico I have often wondered why amongst all the cafés in Santa Cruz it should be this one to which one always returns. One feels no such inner compulsion towards any one of the myriad establishments of Las Palmas. Even when staying up near the Park, where there are several pleasant and better situated pavement cafés, one still finds one's way down here, to sit for ten minutes or for two hours, to see and to be seen. It must be due to its self-generative attraction as a social centre, and to the proximity of the port, of the banks, of the offices of Aucona, the shipping agents for Trasmediterranea services between the islands and back to Spain, and of the shops which purvey the newspapers of Europe some thirty hours after their publication.

The Atlántico will make a convenient centre from which to

TENERIFE

0   5   10

Miles

N

Rocks of Anaga
Anaga
Taganaga
San Andrés
Punta Hidalgo
Monte
de las
Mercedes
Las Mercedes
Bijamar
Tegueste
Santa Cruz
de Tenerife
Valle Guerra
La Laguna
Los Rodeos
Airport
Tacoronte
La Esperanza
El Sauzal
Agua
García
La Mantanza
de Acentejo
Pico de
las Flores
Las Raíces
La Victoria
de Acentejo
Las Galetillas
Santa Ursula
Candelaria
Puerto de
la Cruz
La Orotava
Arafo
Aguamansa
Güimar
Puerto de Güimar
Realejo Bajo
Mirador de
Don Martin
Realejo Alto
La Caleta
San Juan
de la Rambla
Observatory
of Izaña
San Marcos
Mt. Tigaiga
El Portillo
Garachico
Icod de los Vinos
Fasnia
Punta de Dante
Altavista
Refuge
Las Silos
Tanque
Mt. Teide
Montaña Blanca
Poris de
Abona
Buenavista
Las Cañadas
Arico
Punta de Abona
El Palmar
Teno Alto
Santiago de Teidé
Llano de
Ucanca
Guajara
unta
Teno
Cliffs
of los Gigantes
Tamaima
Arguayo
Boca de
Tauce
Chio
Vilaflor
Granadilla
de Abona
Puerto de
Santiago
Guía de Isora
Playa de la Arena
Alcalá
San Miguel
San Juan
Hoya
Grande
Barranco
del Inferno
La Centinela
El Medano
Adeje
Arona
Punta Roja
La Caleta
Los Abrigos
Los Cristianos
Costa del Silencio
Punta de la Rasca

explore Santa Cruz, which although only two-thirds the size of Las Palmas, has a more complex town plan.

We shall first take the road north and east along the coast, a wide promenade overlooking the harbour, which is appropriately named the Avenida de Anaga after the craggy massif of Tenerife's northern peninsula, towards which it leads. After about a mile another great avenue runs into it diagonally: the Rambla del General Franco, which has come right across the city down past the garden suburb, the Park, and the luxury hotels. Shortly after this junction we pass the North Quay where the port ends, and at once come upon a pleasant garden on our right.

The low building behind is the Royal Yacht Club, which like the Casino offers temporary membership to visitors. Those who wish to know what they will be getting for their subscription can make a single free visit on production of a card of introduction from their hotel, gladly provided by hall porter or manager.

This single free visit will be as long as the visitor to Santa Cruz for the odd week will need. He can turn it into a pleasant day's excursion, first giving himself time to see the various old guns displayed outside the adjoining military museum, and especially the cannon named *El Tigre*, the tiger which bit off Nelson's arm in 1797. Then he can enjoy a swim in the Club's excellent pool. And after an aperitif in one of the luxurious lounges he can saunter up to a long lazy lunch in the dining-room with its views out to sea.

But those in Santa Cruz for a month or more may well contemplate temporary membership if they enjoy swimming. For Tenerife is an island of few beaches, of which the capital itself has none. Six miles out along this road, beyond the dirty little village of San Andrés, lies the Playa de las Teresitas, now being developed into a resort; and a mile beyond the Club Náutico stands the municipal baths, which are cheap, but inevitably lack the elegance of the Yacht Club's luxurious *piscina*.

Returning to the Atlántico, if we set off in the same direction but almost immediately take the second street to our left (Calle Villalba) we shall see facing us up some steps on the right the baroque porch of the church of San Francisco. The interior, with a fine altar, has a warm, 'worshipped-in' atmosphere which contrasts with the rather cold atmosphere of many Canary churches.

A few yards beyond is the pleasant square called the Plaza del Principe, which perhaps because several of the best restaurants are nearby, seems to be the hub of activity during the Carnival days of early February. Carnival, more than Christmas or even *Reyes* (the three kings or Twelfth Night) is throughout the Canaries the supreme winter festival. Yet one's memories of the warm nights of celebration are pervaded by a certain melancholy absent from the more tonic air of a Provençal *mardi gras*, and totally alien to the extrovert vulgarity of the German *Fastennacht*.

Even the voices of the masked revellers are muted. For the girls, dressed in their brothers' clothes, and the young men, dressed in their sisters', seek alike to hide their identity in a common high pitched squeak. It is a melancholy every bit as poignant as the melancholy of a Swedish midsummer, for that at least celebrates a real summer, however transient. But *Las Fiestas de Invierno*, as the posters and the lavish programmes describe Carnival, celebrates a winter which, in this land of eternal spring, never comes. As the fancy dress dancers whirl round in the *Circulo de Amistad*, and as the diners stream out from *Gambrinus*, coatless on the midnight air, the almond trees below Santiago del Teide are already in blossom, and there is no relief from colour in the gardens of Orotava.

From the Plaza del Principe run two useful streets: the Calle la Rosa, slightly more commercial, with groceries and dry cleaners, and the Calle del Pilar, with travel agencies and outfitters. And at the top of the Calle del Pilar stands the Park.

Its fifteen luxurious acres amply repay all the water which is expended on them. Whatever the hour of the day or the angle of the sun, one can always find a seat in the shade on one or other of the long avenues where many a white-uniformed Canarian Alice perambulates a dark-eyed Christopher Robin. Visitors will discover for themselves the floral clock just opposite the Calle del Pilar, the ornamental lake, and the zoo alongside the Rambla del General Franco. But I would like to point out to them the hidden circular pergola over towards the left of the Park as we have entered it.

Simply because it is concealed, the four seats around it are often occupied by lovers, but when they are free the backs of these seats deserve a glance. Each is a large painted tile. The first shows Guanches engaged in all the typical occupations of which we have record: milling *gofio*, herding goats, or wrestling, against a background of the valley of Orotava.

The second strongly reminds me of an illustration in the first history book I ever had, in which a group of Anglo-Saxons on some Kentish or Northumbrian cliff watch the arrival of the first Viking longboats. It shows Guanches gravely gazing at three small ships on the sea far below them, and is named 'Arrival of the Conquistadores'.

In the third the invaders and the Guanches are locked in a fierce but as yet unresolved struggle under the tactful title 'Battle of Acentejo'. Tactful, because there were two battles of Ancetejo: the *Matanza*, or Slaughter, which forced the retreat of the Spaniards, and the *Victoria*, or Victory, which led to the natives' capitulation.

The last seat shows us the 'Riches and civilization of the Canaries of today'. 'Today' must have been about 1920. There is a biplane of sorts slowly making its way above what look like paddle steamers in the harbour; but nothing else in the scene would have looked out of place in the nineteenth century.

The ability of glazed tiles to preserve in gleaming anachronism the ephemera of an earlier age is shown even more strikingly in the Plaza 25 de Julio, only a short street away from this side of the Park. Here some twenty seats have been decorated in the same way and at the same period, each by a different firm to advertise its wares. A toyshop shows three dolls such as big girls used to prize when I was a very little boy, looking newer and cleaner than even the Victoria and Albert Museum could have kept them. New Zealand butter was already popular, although the typography of its packets has been streamlined in the meantime. And some vintage car enthusiast must photograph the benches donated by the two great motor importing agencies of the day: Fiat and Buick. They show vast open sedans with long bonnets, with batteries prominent on their protruding steps, and with wheels of many spokes which must have been dust traps indeed on the Canary roads of forty or fifty years ago.

One side of the Plaza 25 de Julio is occupied by the Anglican church, which has a garden of which every English visitor can feel proud. It owes this enviable condition to the care of the English proprietor of the neighbouring Pension Spragg, who himself takes most of the services. In the last chapter I described the Spragg as a Victorian survival, but it is none the worse for that. For a brief moment behind its high wall one is carried back to the days when Britain was Great Britain even beyond the limits of her Empire, when the steamships which called to refuel at these Spanish islands on their way to India, South Africa, the Antipodes, and the British commercial colonies in South America were almost all British

Another hotel under English management in this part of the city was the Pino de Oro, high up beyond the luxurious Mencey. When I first knew it the loveliest private garden in the city surrounded it. A fine dragon tree still dominates the terrace where one took tea, but the grounds have now been sold for development, and in 1971 I watched through binoculars as the beloved old building crashed to the ground.

However there is no lack of lovely gardens in this district. As their best effects are obtained by the splash of vivid colours, especially of bougainvillaea, against white walls, they can be enjoyed from street level, by wandering bemused in the bright sunlight down streets like Calle General Antequera, or indeed almost anywhere to left or right off the Rambla.

Back at the Atlántico we may need something a little stronger than coffee before setting off again, straight up the Plaza de Candelaria this time, and into the bottleneck into which it narrows, the Calle del Castillo. This is the commercial street *par excellence*, with many stores kept by Indians who, with their sari-clad womenfolk, form a small but colourful section of Santa Cruz society. They make good shopkeepers, attentive and all speaking excellent English. But, no doubt for reasons or for profit margins best known to themselves, their establishments all stock exactly the same range of goods: Japanese transistors, oriental leatherwork,

German tape-recorders, English knitwear by manufacturers one has never heard of, cameras, and the *Daily Telegraph*. It is left to the Spaniards to achieve division of labour between butchers, bakers and candlestick makers.

The Calle del Castillo ends in the Plaza Weyler, facing which stands the Captain General's headquarters, from which the whole archipelago was ruled until 1927. From the south-eastern corner of this square leave the *guaguas* and the *micros* for all parts of the island.

It is easy to see why it was chosen as a suitable terminus. For as we proceed on northwards up the Rambla de Pulido and across the roundabout of La Paz up the Avenida General Mola, we are following what before the construction of the motorway used to be the only road out of the capital. In its upper reaches, as it zig-zags round to give breathtaking views of the harbour and the Anaga coast, and pushes out branches towards new housing estates perched high above the city, it is still known as the Carretera General del Norte, the Great North Road.

Such perpendicular expansion was undreamt of in the first centuries after the foundation of Santa Cruz in 1494. The original little settlement grew up, like Las Palmas, beside a dry river bed. Leaving the Atlántico again—we have earned a double whisky this time—and passing in front of and round the General Post Office, we come upon the church of La Concepción, standing beside the *barranco*, a street back from the seafront in a quarter which has rather gone to seed.

Yet this church is popularly referred to as *la Catedral*; and in a chapel in the northernmost of its five seventeenth-century naves hang the proudest relics in the Canaries: the two flags captured from Nelson's landing party in 1797. It was certainly remarkable that little Tenerife with its own levies snatched a victory denied to the might of Napoleonic France. And her achievement was ennobled by the care given to the British wounded, and by the presence over in Las Palmas of the historian Viera y Clavijo, who broke into poetry to celebrate the triumph of his native Tenerife.

The attack was something more than a sporting event, however.

Tenerife

Many eighteenth- and nineteenth-century Englishmen coveted the Canaries, and would willingly have added them to Gibraltar and to our own post-imperial problems. I found a certain lack of tact in the brochure of British United Airways describing its services to the Canaries, which bore on the cover a portrait of Horatio without the arm of which *el Tigre* deprived him.

Crossing the *barranco* and taking the first wide street up to the right, we emerge in front of the market, which is worth a visit even for those who do not come there on a daily shopping expedition. No one can miss the pert flower sellers at the entrance, but after exploring at ground level be careful to go downstairs, where the best of the fruit stalls are to be found.

A few hundred yards behind the market we come upon the *autopista*, the new motorway sweeping down to the seafront, lined in this last stretch with oil companies' premises. Not only is petrol much cheaper in the Canaries than in Spain (5.50 pesetas a litre for premium as against 12.50 pesetas, or 15p a gallon as against 33p), but there is no state monopoly of distribution. The oil companies have gladly jumped into the small but expanding market, and we meet most of the well-known names as we travel round the islands. One has even built a residential estate for its employees about a mile up the *autopista* on the right.

It is up the motorway that we shall drive in order to climb out of Santa Cruz. Even as far as where the road south branches off requires a steep climb, and will do until the new *autopista*, running close to the sea, is blasted out of the cliffs to Candelaria and beyond. And to reach the north of the island this is the only possible route, up to the 2,000 feet high plateau between the massifs of Teide and Anaga, on which, dominating the communications of Tenerife, stands its former capital, La Laguna.

I had toyed with the idea of describing Tenerife under the heads of its native kingdoms, which even today have a certain geographical validity: Anaga, whose rocky coasts first felt the invaders' feet; Tegueste and Tacoronte, whose kings lined up behind the mighty lords of Taoro (Orotava) to repel the aggressor; Icod and Güimar which through caution or through fear of Taoro's hegemony stood aside from the conflict; Daute and Abona about which almost nothing is known, and which even today are the least visited regions of Tenerife; and distant Adeje which once ruled them all. Then I thought of La Laguna, and realized that it was as if I was trying to describe England without taking account of William the Conqueror.

For it is the city of Alonso Fernández de Lugo, the conquistador. Twice he led his forces up to occupy this plateau, and twice retreated to the newly founded Santa Cruz: first after their defeat in the gorge of Acentejo, and again after their Pyrrhic victory on this very spot. Then, after that strange sickness called the *modorra* had reduced the numbers and the vitality of his Guanche foes, his third and last advance penetrated all the way to Taoro, and he founded on the plateau the capital of the newly conquered island: San Cristóbal de la Laguna.

The lake, *la laguna*, which once occupied the shallow depression in the plateau, disappeared long ago as cultivation absorbed its waters, but its name has stuck, while poor St. Christopher is forgotten. The figure who looks like St. Christopher, at the centre of the roundabout where one turns off the *autopista* towards the city, is Father Anchieta, a Jesuit missionary born here in 1534, whose work earned him the title of the Apostle of Brazil.

It is a very Spanish city, not after the Andalusian model, but more essentially Iberian, in the line of those dull little provincial capitals of the *meseta*, where nothing seems to have happened since riches flooded in as men flowed out in the heady days after the fall of Granada and the discovery of America. There are the same sixteenth-century churches with their carved altars (la Concepción, Santo Domingo, and the Cathedral itself, though this last is largely a reconstruction), the same monasteries (San Agustín, San Francisco, and the Seminary, formerly a Dominican monastery, with a dragon tree in its garden), and the same private palaces (Salazar, Nava, and the Bishop's Palace).

There is also the same cold wind of a winter's evening as beneath a light rain one walks between the shuttered white houses down one of the long, deserted streets. The longer amongst these streets seem always to lead to a huge square at the back of the town towards Las Mercedes, on the far side of which a gateway leads to

the most Spanish corner of all. It is the church of the monastery of
San Francisco, and it contains a statue of Our Lord, the Cristo de
la Laguna, which is the object of an intense, Iberian devotion.

The evening that I was there the other members of the congregation were an elderly married couple and four old women. Three
of these at different moments during the service came to the back
of the church and then shuffled forward to the altar on their knees.
Their faces, their expressions, and even the way they wore their
mantillas were more typical of León, of Valladolid, or even of
Soria, than of the Canaries.

I was, indeed, on very Spanish soil. La Laguna is the only place
of importance in Tenerife which does not stand on the site of a
former Guanche settlement. And San Francisco used to be called
San Miguel de las Victorias, in the days when it was here, and not
as today in the Cathedral, that there lay buried the body of Alonso
Fernández de Lugo.

By putting on paper those impressions which have lasted best,
I have perhaps painted La Laguna in unnecessarily sombre colours.
The visitor of half a day may come away with memories of a city
of youth, indeed of some of the most beautiful young people in the
world, moving gracefully in their elegant clothes over the terraces of the monumental University, with unobstructed views of
the Atlantic almost 2,000 feet below.

I am writing these words at a university in northern Europe; and
amidst the cold, the crowding, and the discomfort, I think back
with nostalgia to the wide halls which were so often a refuge from
the sun, to the polished wood of the desks in the library, with
room for all, and to the upholstered armchairs of the amphitheatre.
Nor is the intellect neglected; for several of La Laguna's dons
have international reputations.

For the city has a long intellectual tradition, from even before
the foundation of the *Real Sociedad Económica de Amigos del Pais*
over two hundred years ago. The library and manuscript collec-
tions of this learned society are of immense value to students of the
Canaries. Nor were its early members without practical ability;
they included, for example, the Marquis of Villanueva del Prado
who in 1788 founded the Botanical Gardens of Orotava.

His father had already made the family seat, the Nava palace in La Laguna, a centre of cultural life with his *tertulia*—something between a salon, a club, and a party. In 1757, at the age of twenty-six, the future historian Viera y Clavijo came to live in La Laguna, when his father's promotion in government service brought the family to the capital. In the Marquis's *tertulia* he came to know the other advanced thinkers in Tenerife, and led with them a delightful life of discussions and of country expeditions, when botany and mineralogy were relieved by *ceremoniosas contradanzas* in which the young cleric displayed as light a step as any. The gay clothes, the perukes and the three cornered hats might have served as models for the tapestry cartoons of similar scenes painted by Goya in his earliest, happiest period—but with this difference: that the landscapes where Viera and his friends picnicked, at Agua García or at La Mercedes, were infinitely more colourful and exotic than the banks of the Manzanares.

Inevitably such high-flown speculators had their critics. It says much for the tolerant atmosphere of that golden age of Charles III that a witty attack in 1765 limited itself to gentle sarcasm:

'But now is La Laguna much honoured, with a new assembly which seems like Salamanca. It has chancellor, professors, fellows, and beadle. The chancellor is the Reverend Viera. The professors are the Marquis Nava, the Marquis of San Andrés, and Don Miguel Solís. . . . Never was La Laguna seen with so many wise men as now . . . they attack with the book of Monsieur Voltaire entitled the Gospel of Reason, and the book of Toleration of Monsieur Rousseau. . . .'

Viera was to meet Voltaire in the flesh on the latter's last triumphal visit to Paris. He was also to be present at the funeral of the Empress Maria Theresa in Vienna, and to see most of Europe on a grand tour which lasted from 1770 to 1784, first as tutor to the son of the Marquis of Santa Cruz, and then as a companion to the widowed Marquis himself when after his son's death he wandered from court to court in search of a second wife.

When Viera returned to the islands it was to the cathedral city of Las Palmas as Archdeacon of Fuerteventura (La Laguna was elevated to an episcopal see only in 1818). With his life thus straddling the three largest islands, I would be tempted to call him the most complete *canario* of all if I did not suspect that he was something more. For I believe that he may have been the last informed, utterly aware Spaniard who made his way round the old Europe in the days when his country was still a great imperial power.

His experiments in botany and physics in both Paris and Madrid remind one of his contemporary Goethe, whose first visit to Italy came in 1786. One is reminded, too, of one of his fellow historians, with an even more cosmopolitan outlook, who was writing away at Lausanne during the very period that Viera was working at his *Noticias de la Historia General de las Islas Canarias* (published between 1772 and 1783). It is a pity that they never met, to exchange views in the French which was the common language of the as yet unfragmented society to which they both belonged. Though I hardly dare to voice the thought, I hazard that Edmund Gibbon would have felt himself at least as much at home in the Tenerife of José de Viera y Clavijo as in the England of Horatio Nelson.

Yet I still see La Laguna as a Janus-like city, with on one side youth and high endeavour, and on the other the greedy, ambitious conquistador who has given his title to the main square, the Plaza del Adelantado. (Literally, *adelantado* means 'the advanced one'. It was given to many provincial governors overseas, and to Alonso de Lugo after the conquest of Tenerife.)

One morning Los Cristianos beach, then normally the preserve of the sick and the elderly, was suddenly enlivened by a dozen sylph-like maidens, all laughter and innocence. I found them to be students at La Laguna who had accompanied one of their number, the niece of a local landowner, to spend the week-end at her uncle's country property. A couple of days later I saw the landowner's son, and told him what a breath of fresh air and of beauty his young cousin had brought down with her.

'Yes, they certainly made a change. But it would do them good, too, to get away from La Laguna. It's a terrible place, always rain-ing, always windy, and so high that the thin air makes everyone who lives there slightly barmy.' He went on in this vein for some time.

It was only later that I remembered that his family prides itself on its Guanche ancestry.

The *autopista* continues to the airport of Los Rodeos, the siting of which is one of the bitterest questions in local politics. Everyone in the south of the island will tell you that it should have been placed there, near Güimar or Granadilla, where weather conditions are always perfect and where there is plenty of land which with a little imagination can be described as flat. They will hint that interested parties in Santa Cruz and La Laguna had the ear of the government, as if the Adelantado were still intriguing with Seville and Segovia.

It is true that the plateau of La Laguna is sometimes covered by mist, and that three serious crashes during 1965 (the last involving the death of thirty Swedish tourists on a day trip from Las Palmas) caused the suspension of landing and taking off by night. But the airport was opened when traffic was only a fraction of its present level; the plateau is at least pancake flat; and it is the only site easily reached from both Santa Cruz and the densely populated north coast. Passengers landing in the south would even today require a four hour journey to get to Santa Cruz or Orotava!

Beyond the airport lies the golf course. Beyond this a further stretch of motorway has been completed—eventually it will run all the way to Orotava—parallel to the main road which it has largely displaced.

I propose to rejoin that main road after a detour. Driving north out of La Laguna we pass through the village of Las Mercedes on the edge of the plateau, and then start to climb the mountain which bears its name: Monte de las Mercedes. Although at first it seems the twin of the *monte* on the other side of the plateau, which also takes its name from a village, La Esperanza, they differ in two significant respects. Both are covered by forest. But whereas the Bosque de la Esperanza is of great Canary pines, that of Las Mercedes is of laurel. And the Anaga massif, of which the Monte de las Mercedes forms part, is of older rock, being the remnant with the plateau of Teno in the far north-west of the Tenerife which already existed before Teide.

Three *miradores* or viewpoints have been arranged with parking spaces—and in one case with an inexpensive little restaurant—on the way up. The highest, the Pico del Inglés, at over 3,000 feet, gives views towards Teide in one direction, and right over the Anaga massif in the other. Although a road of sorts continues on a hair-raising route, to link up at San Andrés with the road up the coast from Santa Cruz, the Pico del Inglés is as far as many visitors will choose to venture. From there the eye can wander over an area which despite its proximity to the capital remains one of the remotest parts of the island: towards the crevice leading down to the isolated village of Taganaga, and to the two rocks of Anaga out at sea.

Like the rocks of Salmor off Hierro, these rocks were the last refuge of a distinct species of large lizard; but it is hard to obtain up-to-date information about their present numbers, or even their survival. I was therefore glad to hear from a man of about thirty that in his boyhood on a farm beyond Igueste the Roques were covered with lizards, and that he very much doubted if anything since could seriously have threatened their well-being. He also paid tribute to the keepers of the Anaga lighthouse, who in their leisure hours had taught him to read, and had given him the only schooling he ever had. Thanks to their instruction he was holding down a good job in Santa Cruz.

Returning down the Monte de las Mercedes and turning sharp right when we reach the plateau instead of going on to La Laguna, we drop sharply towards the sea through increasingly fertile country. Leaving Tegueste off the road on our right, we bear right at Tejina and reach the coast at Bajamar.

In travel agency publicity Bajamar figures third amongst Canary resorts after Las Palmas and Puerto de la Cruz. This is because it is conveniently near the airport and the capital, and because it can offer clean modern accommodation under efficient management. Though I would never choose to stay there myself, I may be prejudiced through having always seen it, on my several visits, under a grey cloud and hammered by the Atlantic rollers which made even the much advertised sea water swimming pool unusable.

Bajamar owes much of its cleanness and efficiency to German visitors, who have developed whole estates of chalets which go some way to justify its reputation as a 'German colony'. Though I doubt whether this has any political overtones, I cannot resist repeating the possibly apocryphal story that the developers, as part of their sales talk, urge prospective purchasers to 'buy for the fatherland!'

Two miles further on, where the road dies, lies Punta del Hidalgo, for the last ten winters of his life the refuge of the writer Henry Savage, and still undeveloped. It owes its puzzling name, which means 'promontory of the nobleman,' to the bestowal of this cape on the bastard son of Tinerfe el Grande, the shadowy ruler of the whole island, whose nine sons divided his realm between them. There were thus nine kingdoms ruled by kings, or *menceyes*, in addition the little Punta del Hidalgo. Viera y Clavijo tells a delightful story of how the great *mencey* Bencomo of Taoro visited the Hidalgo on foot and alone, to remonstrate with him for goat stealing, and coming upon him in his cave was invited, in accordance with the Guanche laws of hospitality, to share his meal in a kingly simplicity which out-Homers Homer. When the Spaniards landed, the Hidalgo led his little band to join those of Taoro, Anaga, Tegueste and Tacoronte in resistance.

It is towards Tacoronte that we now travel, returning through Bajamar and Tejina, and then across the banana plantations of the flowery Valle Guerra. It is worthy of mention not only for its red wine, but also for its seventeenth-century convent of San Agustín which contains the Genoese carved wood Cristo de Tacoronte of the same period, and for its church of Santa Catalina with fine silver of Canary workmanship.

Now begins a magnificent stretch of road with views of the peak of Teide on the left, and of the sea far below us on the right. Down there new developments are in progress at Mesa del Mar and at El Sauzal, in a pocket said to be better protected and freer of cloud than anywhere else on the north coast. It is slow driving, with many twists and turns and several villages to pass through, notably La Matanza de Acentejo and La Victoria de Acentejo, the significance of whose names we already know.

Shortly after Santa Ursula the road divides, and whichever branch we take sooner or later presents us with a glorious view of the valley of Orotava in its entirety, sweeping up from the sea to the chain of Tigaiga opposite, and all the way to the white majesty of Teide. However, 170 years ago the right-hand road did not exist. So that it was from the one to the left, which leads directly to the Villa de Orotava (Bencomo's *Arautava*), that the naturalist Humboldt in 1799 gazed on what he later described as the most beautiful prospect of all his travels.

The brevity of his six-day stay in Tenerife, together with a certain disappointment which many feel as they gaze over the monotonous green expanse of banana plantations, has led to some scornful comments on his taste. But the banana is a relative newcomer to the Canary economy. In Humboldt's time the valley offered a panorama of mixed vegetation, with perhaps even more flowers than today. In so far as there existed a dominant crop, this was the vine, from which came the Canary sack which from before Shakespeare's time had been exported to England from Puerto de la Cruz.

It is time that we braced ourselves to face Puerto de la Cruz, whose skyscrapers have in fact been facing us on and off for some miles, appearing and reappearing far below us like some nightmare mirage reflected across the Atlantic from Miami. The approaches to it are still beautiful. Whether we go by the lower road past the Botanical Gardens, or up by Villa Orotava and down past the lovely grounds of the Hotel Taoro, our way through the bananas is lined with jacarandas, tulip-trees and poinsettias. But then Puerto de la Cruz was itself still beautiful when first I visited it in 1960. Then only one hotel had arisen on the as yet uncompleted promenade. Then the beach, though narrow and black, was at least genuine—it has now been extended artificially! Then the shady central square was still a leisurely place in which to spend a quiet hour. Then the old balconied house of the Iriarte, at the corner between the street of that name and Calle José Antonio, which gave to eighteenth-century Spain four sons who were at once servants of her government and ornaments of her language, seemed not wholly alien to the world into which it had survived.

Then, when a few minutes' walk brought one out of town to quiet, flower-lined roads, it was possible to forget Puerto's two great disadvantages: firstly, that the sea is almost always too rough to swim in, and secondly, that about half the days in winter are cloudy. It feels wonderful to sunbathe by the San Telmo swimming pool as the sun glints on Teide's snows 12,000 feet above. But in my experience you can only do it about three and a half days a week.

Now these two disadvantages have been reinforced by many others. For Puerto's growth has been not merely mushroom, but fungous, in the worst sense. Economics and sheer demand for accommodation have no doubt dictated the glass and concrete of the vast new hotels, horribly though they clash with the Canary architectural tradition, which was nowhere stronger than in the valley of Orotava. Even so, these carbon copies of American hotels would be tolerable if they were run with American efficiency, and if their cooking, however monotonous, at least reached the lowest common denominator of agreed international palatability.

It was towards France and Italy that most travellers went before 1914, and between 1919 and 1936 the high standing of the peseta made Spain relatively expensive. So that when the tourists began to flood towards the Costa Brava and Majorca in the early 1950s the country was short not only of hotels but of trained hotel staff. With every year the position has worsened, for while more than three hotels are opening every two days, all the best cooks, barmen and chambermaids are leaving Spain for the higher wages of London, Paris and Düsseldorf. The kindly boy who takes fifty minutes to bring the meat course is doing his best, but a white coat doesn't make a waiter. It is certainly a pity that another quarter of an hour goes by before you can persuade him to produce the mustard, but down on the banana plantation he's never seen the stuff. You must expect the steak, now that you at last have it, to be badly cooked, for the chef had never used a grill before coming here. All they had at home were two little butane gas rings, and the only meat they ever cooked on them was an occasional boiled fowl when one of the hens had stopped laying.

Tenerife

However enraged your feelings may be as the minutes tick by in the crowded stuffy dining-room, while the sunshine for which you have come all this way pours down outside to no purpose, do try to control them. Leave the shouting to that red-faced German at the next table. His language is better suited for it. (For one result of the great simplification of English during the centuries when our ruling class spoke French is that we can only curse in four letter words.)

He is a good example of the 'many other disadvantages' of Puerto de la Cruz, whose number in a year runs into six figures. Resorts tend to attract the tourists they deserve, and the palaces of Puerto de la Cruz are filled with the *poseurs* of the *seizième arrondissement*, the over-fed, over-dressed beneficiaries of the *wirtschaftswunder*, and pleasant, puzzled English couples who wish they had put off their holiday a couple of months and gone to Eastbourne.

In case you are in their position, and are already established at Puerto de la Cruz before you read these lines, let me reassure you that all is not lost. There is a certain amount of cultural life. La Laguna University organizes a gentle course for foreigners there from mid-January to mid-March each year. There are a couple of art galleries, and several artists have made it their centre—although the best of these, Luis Ibañez, always seems to make for the interior or the south when he needs inspiration. And there are some places nearby where you can still enjoy the Canarian *douceur de vivre*.

The first of these is almost immediately at hand, like an oasis amidst the construction sites and scaffolding. It is the pleasant residential district at the top of the hill, around and beyond the Hotel Taoro, the one luxury establishment where there still lingers the charm of an older world. For there was an earlier, less strident invasion of Puerto de la Cruz, by invalids in search of health, and by retired colonial servants seeking winter sunshine. They are recalled by the faded gold *Orotava* over many a garden gate and doorway of Betjemanesque suburbs. And here they have left three enduring memorials.

One is the English church, which both in its services and its congregation takes me back to the well-filled Bournemouth churches of the early 1930s. Then there is the British Library, most of whose 16,000 volumes (it is the largest non-official English library outside the English speaking world) take me back to the turn of the century. And finally there is the delightfully situated British Sports Club on the other side of the main road, whose atmosphere might be that of eighty or ninety years ago. As I took tea the Atlantic far below sparkled blue beyond the croquet lawn; and a lady in linen hat and long pleated white skirt, with a blouse which certainly *looked* as if it had leg-of-mutton sleeves, leaned on her mallet and hailed a dear old gentleman in blazer and panama hat:

'Well played, Colonel Carruthers.'

They might almost have been contemporaries of Mrs. Olivia M. Stone, whose book *Tenerife and its six satellites* helped to increase the numbers of that first tourist invasion. She and her husband spent five months in the islands in the winter of 1883 to 1884—the same amount of time that I spent there in the winter of 1965 to 1966. Their combined expenditure, London to London, at £183 9s 7d, was only a few pounds less than my expenditure for myself alone from Saint-Malo to Saint-Malo. I would have expected prices to have considerably more than doubled over eighty years. It is true that my motor caravan gave me substantial economies, but I had to transport it from and back to Europe, and between the three islands to which it accompanied me. And Mrs. Stone, too, did a lot of camping.

The answer probably lies in the improvements in communications. Good distribution now enables one to purchase everything one needs at more or less standard prices everywhere. And the excellent service of mail steamers from one island to another has put an end to waiting for days at an obscure fishing village for an uncertain schooner whose captain drove a hard bargain for an uncomfortable passage. On the other hand Mrs. Stone's budget must have been helped by the large amount of hospitality she received, especially in the smaller islands where an Englishwoman was in those days a novelty (she claimed to be the first ever to set foot on Hierro).

In Puerto de la Cruz she met 'Mr. Reid, the courteous vice-consul'; and his family, one of whom is still vice-consul, continue to live in the lovely district I have been describing. 'Don Pedro' Reid found his way to Las Palmas in 1862, and moved across to Puerto two years later. The banking and merchanting firm which he founded just a century ago (in 1867) still flourishes. And as my friends David and Heather Reid have now started a family, we can be sure that something of the true character of Puerto de la Cruz will survive.

Only a little further away than the district round the Taoro are the Botanic Gardens. The foundation of these 'Gardens of Acclimatization' as a half-way house for plants of all kinds from the Spanish tropical possessions, in the generally vain hope that after a few years they would be ready to face the climate of Europe, was one of the last acts of the wise Charles III in the year of his death, 1788. They repay a visit even by anyone not particularly interested in botany or gardening.

Four miles and a thousand feet above Puerto—which in origin was a port, and nothing more—lies the capital of the valley, Villa de la Orotava. Amongst several fine houses and monuments is the eighteenth-century church of La Concepción, with a convoluted façade after the style of Churriguera.

About the same distance to the west of Puerto lie the twin villages of Realejo Alto and Realejo Bajo, which stand on the sites of the camps (*reales*) of the armies of Alonso de Lugo and of the Guanches when these surrendered in September 1496. The church of Santiago in Realejo Alto, begun in 1498, marks the spot where Bencomo and his fellow *menceyes* were baptized.

San Juan de la Rambla, five miles further west, has a fine paved terrace dominating the sea, and, like Orotava and the Realejos, several old houses. But for views, for old houses, for the Canaries as I imagined them long before I first went there, it is necessary to travel seven miles east again, to Icod de los Vinos.

This is the place on the north coast where I would myself choose to stay. There are gardens round the great church with benches and a café. There are quiet streets whose houses bear elaborately carved wooden balconies. Two miles below lies the small but safe beach of San Marcos, to which a single bus chugs backwards and forwards all day. Its black sand is now overlooked by two or three blocks of furnished apartments. But I have always encountered flies down there, and would prefer to stay in the clean new hotel just outside Icod called the Hostal del Drago.

It is aptly named. Those who know that they will at some point pass through Icod need not go out of their way in order to look at a dragon tree anywhere else. For here, just beside the road, stands the largest and the oldest *drago* of them all, in a small park which enables it to be seen and photographed from every angle. Though the estimate of its age at 3,000 years may be an exaggeration, it has almost certainly spent more of its life under the Guanches than under the Spaniards.

Garachico, three miles on, was never as is sometimes claimed the capital of the island; but before 1706 it was the most important town on the north coast. It can be approached along the coast road cut between steep cliffs and the sea, or by the upper road from Icod past the dragon tree and by a precipitous narrow descent to the right through the village of Tanque. The second route is longer, and requires some careful driving. But it offers a wonderful view of Garachico from above, when its tiled roofs give it the appearance of a terracotta toytown in which we can pick out the miniatures of the monuments we shall later be visiting. These include the sixteenth-century castle of San Miguel on the seafront, with its emblazoned doorway; the church of Santa Ana; the disused and decaying convent of San Francisco, with two cloisters each with two storeys, which can be visited on application to the town hall; and the still occupied convent of Santo Domingo, where I searched in vain for its turnstile, that ingenious device used by the more enclosed orders to communicate with and to receive supplies from the outside world.

Once there were many more monuments, but they were overwhelmed as utterly as Pompeii in the eruption of 5th May 1706, which not only destroyed the greater part of the town, but by filling in the harbour made its economic recovery impossible. The steepness of the surrounding heights emphasizes its vulnerability to a descent of lava, but it nevertheless owes to volcanic action its

17. Tenerife: carved balconies of the Canary architectural tradition in La Orotava (pp. 124 and 127)

18. Tenerife: dragon tree in the garden of La Laguna seminary (p. 116)

19. Tenerife: the jagged chain of Anaga rising behind the harbour of Santa Cruz (p. 107)

20. Tenerife: another view of Santa Cruz harbour (p. 107)

21. Tenerife: above the valley of Orotava (p. 123)

22. Tenerife: the towering peak of Mount Teide overlooks Las Cañadas (p. 146)

two most distinguishing features. These are the Rock of Garachico out at sea; and the deep fissure in a promontory of lava which forms a safe natural swimming pool and at the same time transmutes the great rollers into moderately sized waves. One can therefore swim with security but without losing all the fun—a possibility offered nowhere else except by a swimming pool with artificial waves in Bucharest.

Beyond Garachico the mountains retreat a little to leave a small coastal plain, which besides bananas grows excellent coffee. Amidst this plain lie the village of Los Silos and the small town of Buenavista, which has for long been the end of the road, with the good views which its name would lead us to expect.

A tunnel, however, has now been pierced through the steep cliff which shuts Buenavista in to the east, and a road is being built along which it will be possible to drive all the way to Punta de Teno, the far north-western point of the island, from which the views are better still. Until now the paths to the lighthouse there have been so impracticable that it has to be provisioned by sea from Puerto de Santiago on the west coast. When I was there, a notice in red warned that no one should proceed along the uncompleted road, and I gazed afar at the light which already showed at the end of the tunnel, like Alice looking down the rabbit-hole towards Wonderland. Somehow I had to explore the ancient massif of Teno, once the territory of the *menceyes* of Daute—a name which survives today in a single headland—a land even more mysterious because less visited than its twin the massif of Anaga.

It was easier said than done. My three maps showed several villages up on the plateau, but each map showed different ones. They also showed roads joining them, but I already suspected that these were *caminos*, paths, rather than proper *carreteras*. Some peasants with a donkey told me that the shortest route to Teno Alto was by '*el risco*', but that it was a little difficult for the newcomer to find. As *el risco* meant the cliff face itself, and as not one of my maps showed that particular path, I instead drove inland from Buenavista up a metalled road which climbed 2,000 feet to a high valley. A peasant woman to whom I gave a lift was continuing on foot for about an hour from where the road ended in a scattering of houses called El Palmar. Listening to her description of the temperate fruits and potatoes which she grew, I realized that here, as so often in the Canaries, less than five miles separate the crops of England from the crops of the West Indies.

Before leaving she pointed out the steep path that I must follow on the other side of the valley, and warned me that I could not hope to go there and back in what was left of the day. So I settled for the night in El Palmar, which had the road, with three buses a day from Santa Cruz, and little else. In particular it had no electricity, and as candles and oil lamps appeared in the windows I realized how we have come to take for granted at least an apology for street lighting in the remotest villages of the most primitive lands. It was with difficulty that I picked my way down the unmade street after dark, and I thought that the French Revolution had started all over again when, on turning a corner, I came face to face with people carrying flaming torches to light their way.

This was a suitable introduction to the timeless realm I was to visit on the morrow. Dawn is a short-lived affair in the Canaries. Although I set off before the sun had risen, I had not gone far before it was pouring down on my already hot back. But a long hour later, as I at last came abreast of the plateau, I was glad to have brought a pullover, for I was hit by a wind which was chilling although not cold in itself.

The path ran on the level through Canary pines and round a steep *barranco* which gave glimpses of the sea. I came across a man working on a cultivated patch, and some distance on at last reached Teno Alto, which no one I spoke to up there referred to as anything except 'the village'. Walking down the wide unmade track between its occasional houses, and past the half finished building of breeze blocks which was to be the remote district's first school, the only sounds were from the wind, and from the ragged hens fluttering away at my appearance. In the certainty that I could get a sandwich of some kind I had brought nothing to eat, and was dismayed to learn, at the only shop, that there was no baker, and no supply of bread for another two days.

Still determined to reach the lighthouse, I trudged on beyond the village across a now treeless tableland. It was broken up by several ridges, and I was soon all but lost. After about two miles I passed a couple of empty farmsteads, and then saw an old man and woman moving about outside a third.

'The lighthouse? It's a long way. But turn right at the end of that field, walk straight on, and you'll be able to see it in the distance. No, there's no village down there, although you say it is marked as Teno Bajo on the map. There are just a few empty buildings, and I can never remember anyone living there. Come and have a cup of coffee on your way back.'

At the corner of the field a boy with some goats redirected me, and on the grassy slope where I at last came in sight of the lighthouse far below I found two women looking after some cows. One of them was obviously a little simple. As the lighthouse, clearly, was too far to reach with the time at my disposal, I returned to the welcome and generous offer of a cup of coffee.

'You found your way all right?' enquired the old lady as she ground up the necessary beans in a little coffee mill. 'That boy at the corner of the field is not all there, as I expect you realized.'

I told her that he had seemed perfectly normal, but that one of the women appeared a little odd.

'So is the other. All three of the people you saw are half mad. And all are my children.'

I learnt that her only normal child, a son, had emigrated to Venezuela. Inbreeding is no doubt inevitable on such a remote and inaccessible plateau. The shortage of rain there means poor crops; but the grazing is good, and the goat's cheese of Teno is famous throughout Tenerife. I enquired about it.

'Yes, I have all these here waiting to be taken down to Buenavista, where I expect the merchant will take them on to Puerto de la Cruz.' She pointed to what might have been half a dozen wheelbarrow wheels. 'My wooden mould stamps a flower on the top of each, and I'm told that at Puerto they ask for "the cheese with the flower". Yes, you can certainly purchase one if you wish: it will be one less to carry down *el risco*.'

With an improvised but ancient balance she weighed my cheese with the aid of a series of stones. I was to enjoy the taste of Teno, a delicious distillation of wind and solitude in crumbly off-white, for long after it had bumped on my back down the steep path back to the outer world.

Just as the road from Santa Cruz to La Laguna and Tacoronte follows the 'pass' between the central massif of Teide and the older massif of Anaga, so there is a road across the north-western corner of the island which follows the similar 'pass' between the central massif and the other older massif, Teno. We have already travelled part of this road on our way to El Tanque in order to enjoy the view of Garachico from above. Now we continue along it, journeying from sub-tropical through Mediterranean cultivation to a Connemara-like country up at Erjos, and finally to an almost Pennine-bare landscape before we go through a narrow cutting and at once find all the west of the island beneath us.

The comparison which leaps to mind is with the west of Gran Canaria. Further down there are even the same almond trees blossoming unseasonably in late January. But in Tenerife the peak overshadows all, and the first village we come to bears its name— Santiago del Teide. Opposite its curious white mosque-like church a stony track winds up towards two other remote hamlets of the tableland of Teno. Although marked on some maps as a road it should be avoided by anyone on wheels.

But then the entire road system south of Santiago should be approached with caution. It has been rapidly improved. There is no longer a dusty, bone-shaking gap from Playa de la Arena, with its sandy beach but fierce sea, through the two slightly larger but equally primitive fishing villages of Alcalá and San Juan. But the development of a resort at Acantilados de los Gigantes, where Teno meets the sea in a series of giant cliffs, has led to the deterioration of what used to be a well-surfaced road from Santiago down to its dirty little port.

From San Juan a good road runs up to the high-set inland town of Guía de Isora, and then north towards Santiago again. Indeed from Chio there are two parallel roads: one via Tamaimo and one via Arguayo. And just where the two separate is the beginning of a third road, which when finished will run up to Las Cañadas, the flat roof of the island, and provide the quickest route from the far west to Santa Cruz. The first few miles down from Las Cañadas, and the first few miles up from Chio already exist. I have followed them both to where they end in utter loneliness, the latter amongst pines with the shape of Gomera across the water, and behind, the white peak which here seems so near.

Work is in progress on a highway from Guía de Isora to join up near Adeje with the road from the capital to the south. This last ten mile link in the circular tour of Tenerife will slice across the island's largest estate managed as a single unit. Some seventeen square miles hereabouts have been British owned for more than a century: and although the style of living at the great house at Hoya Grande in no way conflicts with Canary traditions, an English taste is evident in the lovely gardens around it, and in the siting of the manager's new summer home overlooking the estate's own little port at La Caleta.

For me these western slopes will always be associated with Desmond and Dorothy Goode, who came from deepest Devon to identify themselves with this remote area, studying the folklore as well as farming at every altitude from sea level to 7,000 feet. Below their garden terraces at Hoya Grande lay the plantations of bananas and tomatoes. Far above lay the pine forests. It was Desmond who, in order to permit communication between these extremes, first drove a *pista* down from Las Cañadas to the west coast.

There is another figure too, whom this area brings to mind: the legendary Tinerfe el Grande, who from Adeje is said to have ruled the whole island to which he gave his name. The last part of the story sounds like a transparent invention, and it appears much more likely that *tener-*, snow, *-ife*, mountain, was the name given to the largest island on their horizon by the inhabitants of La Palma.

But that distant dry Adeje should ever have enjoyed pre-eminence seems so far-fetched that for this very reason I suspect that there may be a grain of truth in the tradition. And gazing up at those golden western slopes I have tried to imagine them a century before Alonso Fernández de Lugo landed, before even Béthencourt had sighted Lanzarote, or the Virgin had appeared at

Candelaria. Then, when the pines came down to the 1,000 foot contour, this must have been the best and the largest stretch of uninterrupted grazing on the island. The shepherd king of such a realm must have been a patriarch amongst shepherd kings. Could not the legendary shattering of Adeje's overlordship two or three generations before the conquest have been due to the growth of agriculture in the more fertile north, as fresh techniques were introduced by visiting Europeans?

Adeje has a place in history even without Tinerfe el Grande. It became the seat in Tenerife of the Counts of La Gomera, who at one time had a thousand negro slaves working their land here. No Negroid characteristics survive amongst the present population, however, in contrast to the coastal districts of Gomera itself, where wide jaws, thick noses, and darker skins blend not unattractively with native and Iberian elements. The *Casa Fuerte*, or 'strong house' of the Counts was designed for the protection not only of themselves, but of all this south-western corner of the island. This fortified mansion, after a severe fire, is now a mere shell; but the adjoining farm, divided between two families, preserves a pair of iron cannon balls together with the largest of the sixteenth-century pieces of artillery which used to fire them. I was told that it proved too heavy to remove when the lighter pieces were taken to be melted down during the Civil War.

The quiet, shady little town, the choir of whose church is lined with unexpected Gobelins tapestries, has grown up naturally at the mouth of the deepest and narrowest *barranco* in the islands, the one place where water was always to be found in this dry southwest. But it is the fearsome gorge rather than the green shade which has inspired its name: the Barranco del Infierno. The cascade at the valley head has been channelled into a concrete gallery which winds about half-way up along the northern wall, and the path alongside forms the easiest route up the valley. The water course can not only soothe a heated brow, but provides proof—very welcome after two or three hours without seeing a living soul—that other human beings have passed there. I found an almond tree, perhaps self-sown, with its nuts scattered on the ground unharvested.

Tenerife

National characteristics change little over the years. I have always felt that our own gravest fault is an inability to keep our opinions to ourselves. Documents of the Inquisition show that sixteenth- and seventeenth-century Englishmen were no better. Amongst several cases involving our compatriots in Tenerife alone I noticed that of Duarte (i.e. Edward) Monox, who arrived at Adeje as captain of the *Perocles* with a cargo of sugar. He was brought before the Inquisition on 10th September 1604 for having maintained in public and in private conversations heretical opinions on images, the Papacy, and other points of doctrine.

Long ago I would have saluted Edward Monox as a martyr, but I have since seen too many of his successors pontificating over their third or fourth *coñac*. 'I don't agree with worshipping the Virgin Mary.' 'I don't like Franco.' Let them mind their own business. The Inquisition knew perfectly well that it was only a short step from speaking against images to smashing images, of which John Sanders was accused on 9th February 1565. They knew too that heresy sometimes went hand in hand with other misdemeanours. Thus Bartolomé Coello (i.e. Bartholomew Cowell) of Barnstaple, imprisoned for Calvinism in 1592, confessed to the additional crimes of contraband and sabotage.

The port where the *Perocles* cast anchor was probably Los Cristianos, the island's one harbour worth the name after Santa Cruz itself. It was here that a small detachment of De Lugo's forces landed at the end of the conquest to receive the capitulation of Adeje. For two centuries the danger of privateers, and for another two centuries local politics, in turn prevented the emergence of a second port to take even a little traffic from the capital, no less than sixty-six miles away.

Now at last Los Cristianos is growing, and is already bigger than Adeje or than Arona, the little town up in the hills on which it still officially depends. The reason for its growth is tourism, but what now brings the visitor is the same as what ought in the past to have brought the ships. Surrounded by a semi-circle of bare brown hills and facing west, it is sheltered from the winds which so often make life unbearable at other southern beaches, such as El Médano. And the force of the Atlantic rollers is broken firstly by the headland of the Camisón, and then by the jetty, to produce on at least twenty-eight days a month a calm bay fringed by golden sand on which the sun beats down.

In claiming twenty-eight days of wind-free sunshine a month I make no exception of February. Storms in the Canaries generally come in March, and even then are but a pale shadow at Los Cristianos of the destructive tempests of the north coast. Twice I have stayed there the whole of February and have swum three times every day. I entered the water first at a few minutes past eight, when the sun appeared over the Mountain of Guaza. Then I used to have a longer bathe at midday, when the sixty or seventy expatriates had taken up their regular positions on the beach. And my final dip came late in the afternoon, when Gomera was already changing colour, and when distant Hierro might soon appear briefly outlined against the sunset.

In the light of this sunshine, in a climate not so much of *primavera eterna* as of *verano eterno*, the one criticism of Los Cristianos, 'there is nothing except the beach,' has little validity. One wants nothing else; and though lights in the smaller centres of the Canaries are too dim for sustained reading, the evenings pass quickly over a glass of wine at Manolo's bar with Mr. and Mrs. Brown and Kristina Lafquist, or with the occasional visit to a (generally quite recent) film at the *Ciné Marina* for less than a shilling. Soon there will be all too much to do. A luxury hotel is about to join the simple friendly Hostal Reverón: the three days old *Daily Express* can already be purchased at Enrique's general store. A hundred more tourists will suffice to crowd the beach uncomfortably, and in a few years perhaps the only relic of the blessed isolation I once knew will be the difficulty in getting any sound from the radio. For Teide blocks all the European, and even the Canary transmitters, and I was reduced to picking up such snippets of general news as Radio Senegal chose to send out from Dakar in a fruity French more high-flown than anything heard in Paris.

Small though the beach is, and inbred the society of foreign residents which has collected there, Los Cristianos is the only worthwhile place for a winter holiday anywhere on the southern or eastern coast. Though they will figure increasingly in travel agent's brochures, I intend to dismiss in a very few lines the resorts which are being developed.

At Las Galletas a landowner for whom I nourish a fond admiration has joined with Belgian capital (hence the name of the development company, *Ten-Bel*, meaning Tenerife—Belgium) to build the estate called Costa del Silencio. From many of the well-built houses there are fine views over a foreground of rocks and *euphorbia* towards Teide. But the swimming is directly from the low cliffs, down ladders into the heaving swell.

Los Abrigos, the next potential resort, is at present simply a dirty little fishing village. But beside the coastal track between there and that red rock landmark, the headland called the Punta Roja, lie two beautiful and deserted beaches, El Confital and La Tejita. On the day I visited them there was only a moderate wind.

Beyond the Punta Roja stands El Médano, with an equally good beach, but swept whenever I have been there by a blast which has made swimming or sunbathing impossible. Those who know the place better assure me that calm days are not unknown, but they also assure me that they are not typical. Such little local life as gives it character is imported down the steep but well-engineered road from the commercial centre of the south, Granadilla. I was interested to find in 1971 that El Médano, the first place in the south to be developed, had hardly grown in five years.

The full name of Granadilla is Granadilla de Abona; and the name of the most obscure of the old Guanche kingdoms is recalled again by Poris de Abona and the nearby Punta de Abona, fifteen miles up from El Médano as the crow flies (twenty-five by road). The lonely beachless coast with its low cliff has a certain dim beauty. The village is as dim as the memory of Abona itself. I believe that the coast between here and Puerto de Güimar is equally uninspiring, although I only know it from travelling along it a few hundred yards offshore. The maps mark a number of beaches, but only one can be approached by road. It must be remembered, too, that many Canary *playas* can be sand today, and shingle or even rock after a night's storm.

From this depressing coastal survey it is a relief to turn inland, and in particular to the highroad to Santa Cruz which follows roughly the 1,500 feet contour at from three to eight miles from the sea. This is in itself depressing to anyone who drives along it frequently, for it contains no straight stretch of more than two hundred yards in all the sixty-six miles from Los Cristianos. Some claim almost a hundred twists and turns, others more than a thousand. It all depends on how big they have to be to qualify for counting. The bigger ones are due to the many *barrancos* which the road can only negotiate by following them in to the point where they are narrow enough to be bridged.

The motorway to the south has shortened the journey. But it has also ended a mental experience, a study in brown, a view of the world at an angle of thirty degrees, in which candelabra cacti, and little white towns beyond *barrancos*, and storage caves, and the sea far below, and the occasional dark suggestion of pine forests far above, are alike remembered in a sienna haze. The haze exists only in the memory, for visibility is never less than excellent in the south of Tenerife.

There are two *miradores* from which, thanks to this visibility, much of the south can be surveyed. The first, beneath the rock called La Centinela, the Sentinel, allows us to see much of the landscape from the Punta Roja to Chayofa. This last place is the headquarters of Don José Tavio, on whose land lies the Costa del Silencio. A keen local patriot, he has conducted more than one minister from Madrid over the potato fields, the tomato plantations, and the cucumber gardens made possible by the water galleries, over his packing stations and estate developments, and even over the mock airfield which he has already laid out in white lines as a broad hint of what the south needs and of where it ought to be.

Legend has it that the cavalcade of cars then winds up to Chayofa, a welcome splash of colour amidst the brown, past the only petrol station I know that is wreathed in bougainvillaea, between the huge earthenware urns planted with geraniums, to a great white hall with many windows, the largest building for many miles. Here, surely, the patrician holds court. Here will be prepared the banquet to close the day. It is already past three, late for lunch even by Spanish standards, and the minister's lips move in anticipation. And when the great doors are flung open a banquet is indeed revealed, already taking place. In a double line of stalls the finest milking herd in Tenerife is chewing the cud.

The countryside we dominate from La Centinela was the last in Tenerife to see an eruption (Chinyero, 1909). It seems hard to imagine volcanic forces so near the quiet clean little town of San Miguel, the line of whose houses and trees appears beyond the *barranco*. But that eruption cost no lives, whereas twenty people died at the next town, Granadilla, when in 1961 the town hall collapsed through mere old age.

Granadilla is an important junction. Apart from the main highway running through it and the road which drops to El Médano, it is the terminus of the southern route up to Las Cañadas, which it enters by a gap in the crater wall called the Boca de Tauce. About half the distance from Granadilla to the Boca de Tauce, and midway in altitude between them, stands the highest village in the archipelago, the beautifully named Vilaflor (flower town). At 4,800 feet it is a beautiful place in its own right. Below it lie terraced fields cultivated on a system resembling Lanzarote's, whereby they are spread with a layer of sand to attract the dew.

Amongst their crops are vines, from which comes the best known white wine of Tenerife. It can be purchased 'loose' from any of the bars, and from many other houses. Although more than twice the price of the white wine of Lanzarote, it is not, to my taste, as good. I had a bottle of each side by side, and was able to make a direct comparison such as few have the opportunity of doing. Purely on its own merits it is pleasantly dry, and not altogether unlike *manzanilla*.

Above Vilaflor stretches one of the most extensive of the series of Canary pine forests which form a continuous but uneven ring between the 4,000 and 7,000 feet contours, between the cultivated lands below and the deadland of Las Cañadas beyond. Because of its drier climate it is not as dense as the better known forest of La Esperanza. But it contains some fine trees, one of which, 200 feet high, has the record for girth of the species, being about nine feet wide. Its distance from the capital, and the immense view down towards the Punta Roja and the Punta de la Rasca make it the loneliest and my own favourite Tenerife forest. The combination of height, sunshine, and resin scented air should make Vilaflor a healthy place to stay, although I have never met anyone who has done so.

To reach the second of the two *miradores* of the south we must travel thirty miles on from Granadilla along the main road, through Guanche-sounding hamlets like Chimiche and Icor, which incongruously send off sacks of potatoes to stand in many a market and greengrocery of midland England. The *mirador* of Don Martín stands where the great brown slope of the east coast is dramatically interrupted to leave a gentle shelf which by contrast appears as a coastal plain.

It is easy to see why the *mencey* of Güimar ranked second in power only to the *mencey* of Taoro, for their valleys were complementary, one to the south and one to the north of the main range. Inevitably that of Güimar is drier, and as the pleasant but uninteresting town of Güimar itself is sheltered round more than a hundred and eighty degrees by encircling mountains, it is both sunny and protected from the wind. It is surprising, therefore, that no foreigners stay there, especially as moderate numbers did winter there in the early years of the century.

So much depends on the presence of a good hotel, and writers of that generation sang the praises of a comfortable, isolated, and now, alas, forgotten establishment at Güimar called the Buen Retiro. However, a modern hotel has now arisen at the *mirador* of Don Martín itself.

From their bedroom terraces its guests will be able to look down not only on Güimar but across at Arafo on the other side of the valley, which produces a white wine preferred by some to that of Vilaflor. In the middle of the plain they will observe the baby volcano called the Montaña de Güimar, over 900 feet high despite its toytown appearance from the *mirador*. Though this volcano hides much of the coast, they will have a glimpse of the little port of Güimar, which like Puerto de la Cruz may find a larger role when the southern motorway is driven through. Be-

yond the Montaña de Güimar they will see the much steeper coastline running all the way to Anaga; and although Santa Cruz itself
is invisible they will recognize its position by the great ships
standing out at sea.

Then, lowering their eyes a little to where the cliffs begin and
the coastal plain ends, they will become aware in the distance of a
building larger than any in the town of Güimar, and bigger indeed
than many public buildings in Santa Cruz. They will be gazing at
the shrine of Our Lady of Candelaria, patron not only of Tenerife
but of the Canary Islands as a whole.

Fatima and Lourdes owe to the appearance of the Virgin their
elevation from remote villages to world pilgrimage centres. In
choosing Candelaria for a visitation, on the other hand, she was
paying tribute to the importance already possessed by Güimar in
pre-conquest times. For her statue was discovered standing on a
rock near the sea by two Guanche herdsmen late in the fourteenth
century, a full century before the invasion of Tenerife by the
Spaniards. One of them threw a stone at the mysterious figure
when she refused to answer him, and found his offending arm
paralysed. This evident power, her beauty, and the mystery of her
arrival caused the *mencey* Damarmo of Güimar to summon all eight
of his fellow kings, who agreed that she should be placed in a cave
on the site of the present basilica, where she became the object of
veneration throughout the still pagan island.

In 1464 Sancho de Herrera, of the family who by now ruled the
four lesser islands, seized the statue and carried her off to Fuerteventura. Every morning there she was discovered with her face
turned to the wall, and when in addition a plague broke out it was
decided to return her to Tenerife. Thirty years later she was fully
integrated into the church immediately after the conquest, and the
first basilica was built for her early in the sixteenth century. Her
departure was as sudden as her arrival. In 1826 a freak storm
accompanied by a tidal wave carried her out to sea.

The present statue, though only a copy of the lost original,
resembles many fourteenth-century works of the Christian Mediterranean. Whether even at that early date Güimar was already
more friendly towards newcomers, or whether the presence of the

Virgin for over a century disposed its *mencey* against resistance to the Spaniards, the time and place of her arrival could not have been more propitious. The great red stone figures which surround the square outside her basilica represent the Guanches of whom, in a deeper sense than Alonso Fernández de Lugo, she became the conqueror.

The old road to Santa Cruz is particularly precipitous in the first two miles after Candelaria, and winds along a steep slope all the way. It is the counterpart of the steep slope along which winds the north coast road from Tacoronte to Orotava. And between the two, along the very crest of the ridge, runs the most extraordinary road in Tenerife.

We can reach it by turning up the *autopista* and then left at the statue of Padre Anchieta, along the road marked to La Esperanza and Las Cañadas. Beneath the sign is a detachable plaque which normally reads 'ABIERTO' (open), of a type at once recognizable by those familiar with mountainous districts of the Peninsula. It is the only one of its kind in the Canaries, and it is only rarely that it reads 'CERRADO' (closed). But it can do, for we are about to climb to country so high that even at this latitude snow can fall there.

And what a climb! After four miles we pass the village of La Esperanza, and soon afterwards enter all of a sudden the pine forest of the same name, as the gradient increases, bearing us higher and higher above the plain of La Laguna. Another two miles on is a restaurant, with a short road to the left down to a glade where stands a monument.

This is Las Raices, the roots. The name stems presumably from the gnarled roots of the fine specimens of *Pinus canariensis* all around, but a great movement also had its roots here. For in this sylvan setting, where Robin Hood himself would have felt at home, General Franco, then Captain-General of the Canaries, gathered the Tenerife garrison on 17th June 1936, a month before he flew to Morocco and on to Seville at the beginning of the Civil War. The comparison which kept suggesting itself to me, however, during an utterly silent and lonely day amongst the great pines, was not with a gathering of outlaws in the greenwood, but rather with a prayer meeting of the Ironsides before Marston Moor or

Naseby. Not everyone likes Oliver Cromwell, but few will deny that his dedicated career left England a stronger nation.

Barely fifteen miles from the capital, the Esperanza forest is a favourite goal of week-end and holiday excursions, and is criss-crossed by paths and even tracks open to vehicles. There is a fine panorama from the *mirador* of Pico de las Flores, three miles beyond Las Raices. Better views, however, await those who persevere up to the 5,000 feet level and beyond, where the pines are thinning out.

We realize then why this is called the *carretera dorsal*, the back-bone road. For we are now following the crest of the ridge between the two seas. In the absence of trees we are able now to see the coastline far below on either side, towards Orotava on the north and towards Güimar on the south, and generally at least La Palma and Gran Canaria amongst the other islands. Not always, for on overcast days along the north coast this is the cloud level. Here, therefore, as always just beyond the habitat of the pine, lies a belt of moisture-loving vegetation in which predominate two equally indigenous plants: laurel and heather.

Still we climb. The first time I travelled this road I came in the opposite direction; and the sight of the thin line of tarmac winding far ahead with the ground sloping steeply away on both sides made me want to turn back—if I could have found a place to do so. But one becomes used to anything, and this is not in fact a dangerous road.

Practically the only vegetation now is a hemispherical bush sometimes several feet across: the *retama* or broom of Tenerife's lunar uplands. In April and May it flowers, carpeting this seem-ingly dead country with white blossom. Then can be seen every now and again a brown cylinder between the *retamas*, and the silence is broken by a low hum. The bees are busy collecting the famous honey of Teide and storing it in hives which are still made from hollowed palm trunks as by the Guanches.

There are other plants besides the dominant *retama*, notably the *codeso*, *Adenocarpus viscosus*. And at the Llano de Maja, just before El Portillo, at almost 7,000 feet, live the last thirty members of the species of *Serratula canariensis*. The remoteness of its habitat is no guarantee of survival. For it only reproduces slowly, and only develops slowly, and the young plants during their long infancy are killed off by recently introduced insects.

Up on the left we pass the observatory and television transmitter of Izaña, which enjoys a view of the entire east and south coasts from Anaga to the punta de la Rasca. Then we drop a few hundred feet to reach, with as much surprise as Livingstone encountering Stanley, a road junction. This is El Portillo, where the road from Orotava joins us after an even more abrupt ascent, zigzagging from the exotic vegetation of the Botanical Gardens, through the temperate crops cultivated below Aguamansa, up beyond pine and heather to rock and *retama* in less than twenty miles.

Here begins the National Park of Las Cañadas, which although by no means absolutely level is best regarded as a high tableland—an *altiplano* as the Peruvians or Bolivians would call it. After travelling the fifteen miles to the Boca de Tauce we shall be at about the same altitude as when we left El Portillo. We may travel the fifteen miles rather slower than we expect, for the internal combustion engine, like the human body, notices the thin air. From the Boca de Tauce the road drops steeply to Vilaflor and the south, and from there, too, run the first few miles of what when completed will be the highway to the west coast.

This meeting of four routes in Las Cañadas shows Tenerife as the supreme example of a rule which applies in varying degrees to all the islands except the lower, more level Fuerteventura and Lanzarote. This rule is that the shortest way from one point on the circumference to another is across the centre, however high. Even when, as here, this involves a climb of over 7,000 feet, it avoids the time-consuming twists and turns of the coastal roads as they wind round the *barrancos*.

This was evidently realized by livestock graziers from the earliest days of the conquest. For *cañadas* was the word used in the peninsula for the routes followed by the flocks of the *mesta*, the great merino monopoly. The Guanche shepherds, too, knew Las Cañadas, where their earthenware vessels, filled with stores of grain, are even now sometimes discovered hidden. It has been suggested that their owners may have departed hurriedly when the flocks of goats, then as now, made their sudden, inexplicable mass descent to a lower altitude at the turn of the season.

From all this it can be gathered that Las Cañadas are not altogether devoid of life. The *retama* are supplemented in the area near the *Parador* by a daring plantation of pines, which now that goats are forbidden to graze up here may have the success it deserves. In 1964 half the trees had died of drought, for although it very occasionally snows up here it almost never rains. But it is said that woodland in itself attracts moisture, and on my visits two and seven years later I saw far fewer withered brown skeletons amongst the now taller trees.

Men, too, not only pass through but also stay up here. There is a restaurant at El Portillo, and a white sanatorium off the road, like a mirage in a black desert. And there is the *Parador* itself.

It is less adventurous in design than the one at La Cruz de Tejeda in Gran Canaria. But when the last taxi full of tourists from Puerto has left in the late afternoon, and the last lorry returning from Santa Cruz to Granadilla has rumbled eerily away into the immense black shadows over the Llano de Ucanca, the handful of guests settle down to a unique experience. Thrown together with less intention than the members of an Antarctic expedition, they resemble the characters in a novel, caught by chance on some storm-bound Hebridean island or a Shangri-la of science fiction. They converse with increasing frankness round the flaming pine logs as they become hourly more aware of the insulating quality of the utter silence without.

Dawn is as strange an experience as sunset. Waking at 7.30 in my motor caravan, I would find the water from the waste pipe of the sink frozen on the ground. Yet half an hour later, immediately after the sun had risen, I would be eating breakfast in its rays, wearing nothing but a slip and sun-glasses.

There are many square miles, lost to view among the rocks and *retama* bushes, where it is possible to sunbathe wearing even less. With its wonderful air, and the excellent water from the spring at the eastern end of the Llano de Ucanca, I have found Las Cañadas ideal for a few days of utterly simple and perfectly healthy living.

Tenerife

I have not tasted the supreme experience it has to offer: the ascent of Teide. I am assured, however, that this presents no serious difficulties, although the refuge hut at Altavista, up beyond the light-coloured shoulder called the Montaña Blanca, is closed during the winter.

The circumference of the uneven plateau of Las Cañadas is edged by a whole chain of jagged peaks, amongst which Guajara, named after the beautiful sister-in-law of Bencomo of Taoro, is the highest in the Canaries after the 'new' and 'old' peaks of Teide itself. El Portillo and the Boca de Tauce represent the only gaps in this surrounding wall through which roads can be driven up from north and south.

It is a puzzling formation, over-simplified by those who describe it as one vast extinct crater. A more plausible explanation is that it represents the collapsed peak of an earlier and even greater volcano, a 'pre-Teide' of over 16,000 feet. This would have risen at least 22,000 feet from the ocean bed, rivalling Everest in abrupt continuity, and with a peak white all the year. For the lesser Teide that faces us across Las Cañadas today, at 12,152 feet the highest mountain in Spain, lies only 2,000 feet below the perpetual snow line.

How dare I speak of lesser! Although the main reason why I have never made the ascent is that I am not a climbing man, I shall not make it even when that sacrilegious funicular is at last completed. The Guanches recognized gods when they saw them, and showed a proper respect for their own presiding deity.

The transformations in Tenerife after five years have been in the south, where the magnificent new motorway has brought Los Cristianos within a short hour's drive of Santa Cruz. As a result it has ceased to be a village, while other sites—less sheltered from the wind—are being developed along the west coast at Palm-Mar, Playa de las Américas, and Callao Salvaje. Neither these, nor the extensions to Puerto de la Cruz, will be to everyone's taste.

Santa Cruz itself, on the other hand, has been a major beneficiary of the new prosperity. While losing none of its charm, it now has the finest shops in the Canaries, offering a range and quality one never expected to find in the Islands.

6

Gomera

The land across the water exercises a spell which only a visit to it can break. From only twenty miles away Gomera beckoned me during two long stays at Los Cristianos. Once a week a small boat, almost the sole survivor of the many odd services which used to ply between the lesser ports, arrived from Gomera with workers for the tomato fields of south Tenerife, and once with a whole family complete with goats and hens. But when, at the beginning of March, I decided to cross over myself, a storm sprang up the night before the boat was due, and took some days to blow itself out. The macaroon silhouette on the horizon became as desirable as Avalon or Cythera, and as unattainable.

Such anticipation generally leads to disappointment. But though the mail steamer has now carried me there three times, the spell of Gomera is with me still.

I already knew well the greater San Sebastián, the Basque resort which is Spain's summer capital, and realized that San Sebastián de la Gomera would have little in common with it except the name and the sea. To my surprise, however, it shared one other feature: a huge statue of Christ on a hill overlooking the bay.

It seems an extraordinarily quiet and peaceful little town to be the capital of an island which sends so many emigrants to Tenerife and further afield. It is also surprisingly level: as flat as Arrecife and a good deal more flat than Puerto Rosario. For although Gomera's highest point, Alto Garajonay, is lower than that of all islands save the two easternmost, it offers the most difficult terrain of all for communications. The jagged peaks which close the view up the *barranco* of San Sebastián look fearsome enough even before one realizes that they have to be climbed by anyone travelling by road to anywhere else in the island.

For this reason most travel until recently was by sea to the nearest landing point, and then by mule-track into the interior. A road of sorts now zigzags round the north of the island, but Manolo with the *Morrre-e-e-esss verde*, who has replaced Miguel the muleteer, takes four hours to cover the forty miles to Valle Gran Rey—twenty-two as the crow flies. And in the south the important fishing villages of Playa Santiago and La Rajita, linked to the rest of the island only by terrible dirt tracks, still depend upon sea transport for all ordinary business.

This rugged terrain has determined Gomera's past history and its present interest: the development of its unique whistling language, and the survival of a primitive community like Chipude. For in relation to size it has the most eventful history of any of the islands.

A history with tragic moments: there is a menace in that serrated rocky outline behind the quiet town. Hernán Peraza 'the Elder' was aware of this menace when in the mid-fifteenth century he built the squat but solid square stone tower which dominates the bay. Though Béthencourt had claimed to have received the *gomeros'* submission, and later Prince Henry the Navigator had established a Portuguese base in the south of the island, subsequent events show that there had been no true conquest.

John II of Castile secured the withdrawal of the Portuguese by agreement in 1450, and Hernán Peraza, who already ruled Lanzarote, Fuerteventura, and Hierro established himself at San Sebastián. The title of Count of La Gomera was granted a quarter of a century later to his son-in-law Diego de Herrera, as part of his compensation for renouncing the right to conquer the three main islands. But this title did not at first have the same significance as in fifteenth-century Europe. The role of the Conde de la Gomera was nearer to that of the late Roman *comes* from which the title derives. He performed a specified work of defence in return for privileges. His relationship with the islanders was based on the *gánigo*, a native word meaning a pottery vessel, which like the agreement it signified could easily be shattered by ill treatment.

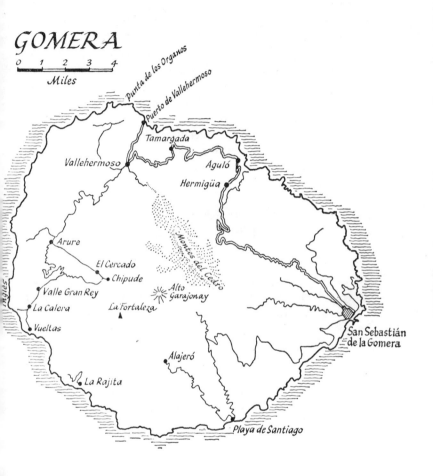

GOMERA

0   1   2   3   4
Miles

Punta de los Organos

Puerto de Vallehermoso

Tamargada

Aguló

Vallehermoso

Hermigüa

Montes del Cedro

Arure

El Cercado

Chipude

Alto Garajonay

Valle Gran Rey

La Fortaleza

La Calera

Vueltas

San Sebastián de la Gomera

La Rajita

Alajeró

Playa de Santiago

Gomera

Difficulty of interpretation led to the succession of disasters which overtook both parties to this uncertain contract. In 1481 Juan Rejón, the disgraced founder of Las Palmas, had so far restored his position at court that he was sent off with two caravels to conquer La Palma. Landing to take on provisions and water at Hermigua on the north coast of Gomera, he was killed by servants of the new Count, Hernán Peraza 'the Younger' (Diego de Herrera's favourite son), who had been ordered to bring him before their master alive or dead.

Gomera is a considerably smaller place than were the Plantaganet dominions, where a similar ill-considered word led to murder in the Cathedral. Had Peraza's authority been more direct such a mistaken crime might never have been committed.

For mistaken it was. Summoned to the court, where he met and married the beautiful heiress Beatriz de Bobadilla (rumoured to be the paramour of King Ferdinand), Hernán Peraza was only pardoned on condition that he led a contingent of *gomeros* to help in the still uncompleted subjugation of Gran Canaria. Pedro de Vera, the governor who had succeeded Rejón at Las Palmas—he had prevented his predecessor from landing there, and had every reason to be pleased at his death—placed him at Agaete where he got on well with the local commander, Alonso de Lugo (see Chapter Four). As in many later campaigns right down to the Civil War, the *gomeros'* ability to communicate by whistling proved invaluable.

Back on his own island, the Count and his bride behaved in such a high-handed manner towards the natives that these had good cause to consider the *gánigo* broken. But one particular incident served as the spark of rebellion. It has come down to us in such circumstantial detail that even its incidentals can be accepted as shedding light on the situation in that remote island almost half a millennium ago.

Not content with one lovely wife, Hernán Peraza took as mistress a beautiful native princess named Iballa, whom he used to visit in her cave, Guahedun, in the west of the island. In anger at her violation, her chieftain father Hupalupa, her brother, and her betrothed, the chieftain Autacuperche, conspired to kill the seducer.

Gomera

As a safe place to plot they chose a low-lying rock about fifty yards offshore from Valle Gran Rey, which has been called ever since 'La Baja del Secreto'. *Baja* is a local word meaning a rock or reef.

After they had agreed on their plans Hupalupa's son expressed a doubt: 'And if the Count finds out?'

His father's reply was immediate and to the point.

'If he finds out it will be through you,' he cried, killing this weak-willed conspirator with a dagger.

The remaining two surrounded the cave of Guahedun with their men on 20th November 1488, while the Count was within making love. Disturbed, Hernán Peraza sought to escape by a mountain track. Iballa, standing at the mouth of the cave, heard the whistled signals of her father's men planning to cut off her lover's retreat. She shouted a warning:

'*Ajel ibes jujaque saven tamarec!* Run, fly, they are going to climb by your path!'

He did not run fast enough, however, and was cut down.

His murderers at once led their forces towards San Sebastián. Beatriz de Bobadilla, informed of what had taken place, had just enough time to send for help to Pedro de Vera, and then shut herself with her babies in the Torre del Conde. This was probably the only existing building in the islands outside Lanzarote capable of withstanding the attack which raged around it for some days, until the relieving forces arrived from Gran Canaria.

Then began a savage repression, in which the natives of Gomera were really conquered for the first time. Many were sold into slavery, although Hupalupa himself is said to have escaped by swimming to Tenerife, then still free. The court, on learning of this brutality, ordered the re-purchase and return of the slaves, and the disgrace of Pedro de Vera.

The implications of this story can best be considered on one of the solid *tea*[1] floors of the tower itself, or on its flat roof, looking out over the bananas which have replaced the sea which helped to protect Beatriz de Bobadilla from the warriors of Hupalupa.

It tells us so much. That prehistoric Gomera was not under a

[1] Heart of pine, a magnificent wood given only by the finest examples of *Pinus canariensis*.

single chief as Viera y Clavijo claimed, but under several—as might be expected from its terrain. We even hear the names of its four tribes: *Ipalan* (San Sebastián), *Armiguad* (Hermigua), *Agana* (Vallehermoso), and *Orone* (Arure). And besides these place-names we are given almost the only complete sentence of any of the native languages to have survived: Iballa's cry of warning to her lover. It is revealing that Hernán Peraza, most of whose life had been spent in Gomera, could evidently understand this cry perfectly, but was unable to follow the whistled signals which had alerted Iballa to his danger. That the island had been occupied but unconquered for so long, and that the enslaved natives were ransomed and returned agrees with anthropological evidence that Gomera has a higher proportion of native blood in its present population than any other island. Finally, Hupalupa's legendary swim to Tenerife (why did he not slip across in a boat?) reinforces the belief that the natives had lost—if they ever had—any knowledge of navigation.

Beatriz de Bobadilla was not the woman to languish in lonely widowhood. Later she was to marry the great Alonso Fernández de Lugo. And already only a year or two after her first husband's murder she was to enter into relations with a man who in the roll of history ranks higher than any governor or conquistador.

I have deliberately used an inconclusive phrase to describe the connection between the Lady of La Gomera and Christopher Columbus. Their liaison may have been purely commercial. On his second voyage, in 1493, for example, the new Noah purchased in San Sebastián all the domestic animals and some of the seeds with which to colonize his Indies.

He no doubt realized the need for these from his years spent in Madeira, which had required similar introductions only a couple of generations earlier. No doubt, too, Gomera attracted him as Madeira had done, as a far outpost to the west. In 1492, when Tenerife and La Palma were still unconquered, it offered the last passable harbour in the Spanish dominions. But in Madeira Columbus had been a married man: when he touched at Gomera he was a widower. . . .

The island's reputation less than four years after its Count's

murder and the savage repression of its fierce native revolt cannot
have been a savoury one. Was the Admiral drawn by some attraction more compelling than its rather poor harbour facilities? It has
recently been proved that Beatriz de Bobadilla was present at the
court of Castile at times when it had been thought that she was
confined by Queen Isabel to Gomera.[1] The itinerant court was by
its very nature a relatively small society, and when there she could
—indeed she must—have met Columbus.

Perhaps they merely discussed his need of provisions, and her
terms for supplying them, in their mercenary fifteenth-century
way. Perhaps, as some authorities have suggested, the social gulf
between them was too wide for their relations to be other than
commercial.

We are still in the Torre del Conde, where their interviews must
have taken place, and we experience a curious sensation even today,
standing in the oldest building in the Canaries still intact and in
use.[2] But what must he have felt like, in the last three storeyed
construction of the known world he was about to leave? And with
what interest must she have listened to this inspired yet practical
man of the world, who, whatever the difference in their social
station, had arrived with the Queen's warrant and as Admiral of
the Queen's ships, to relieve the monotony of her remote island?

He was, after all, a fellow European in a newly conquered
colony. Even today, when the *gomeros* are Spaniards like any others,
and when the mail steamer calls regularly three times a week, you
will soon notice a foreigner in the quiet streets of San Sebastián,
which still follow the regular plan of a later Italian, the royal
engineer Leonardo Torriani. The unhurried proprietors of the
dozen or so shops, all offering a similar range of wares from the
products of Heinz and Liebig to large iron pans for toasting *gofio*,
have plenty of time to question you and to comment on other
outsiders. I was always being told of the English family who used
to sail over in their yacht from Tenerife to the coastal estate they

---

[1] *Cristóbal Colón y Beatriz de Bobadilla en las antevísperas del Descubri-
miento* by Antonio Ruméu de Armas, in *El Museo Canario* XXI 1960.

[2] Although burnt by the Dutch in 1599, its stonework and appearance are surely little changed since 1492.

had bought near Valle Gran Rey. And I was drawn by sheer companion feeling to two women from Berlin who were over to buy land, and who were the only other foreign visitors at the same time as myself. Beatriz must have found in the friendship of the cosmopolitan Italian at the very least a heaven-sent relief from her resentful, gibberish-speaking neolithic subjects.

Columbus, for his part, called here on his first voyage in 1492, on his second in 1493, and on his third in 1498, when she was married again and living in Tenerife. But he conspicuously avoided Gomera on his fourth and last voyage in 1502.

Three other buildings claim connection with the discoverer. A balconied house on the right-hand side of the main street, in a very bad state of repair, is said to be where he stayed. He is also supposed to have been entertained in a much more attractive house, in process of restoration when I was there. Its pleasant patio is entered by a door in a blank wall of the main square, where the usual bandstand in the shade of the laurels has been joined by a surprisingly modernistic café.

Finally the parish church, with greater right than the chapel of San Antonio Abad at Las Palmas, can claim to be the last place of worship where he prayed before casting off on his great adventure. It is a pleasant old building, with some pictures of uncertain attribution and good woodwork bathed in a dim religious light. Its incumbent is generally arch-priest of the eight priests on the island.

As so often, however, the sanctuary which receives most devotion lies outside the town. It is the chapel of Our Lady of Guadelupe, a couple of miles north along the coast, and visible from out at sea long before San Sebastián itself. On her fiesta in October the Virgin is brought to the capital by boat, in the same way that until recently most of her worshippers used to travel round the island.

San Sebastián was the birthplace on 9th November 1757 of Antonio José Ruiz de Padrón, whose career, in its parallels with and differences from that of his contemporary the Abbé Sieyès, sheds a revealing light on the parallels and differences of Spain and France in the late eighteenth and early nineteenth centuries. He

became a Franciscan and in 1784 embarked for Havana, but his
ship was driven on to the coast of Pennsylvania. Reaching Phila-
delphia, the young friar enjoyed a social success, and was invited
to the parties both of Franklin and of Washington. Wishing to
travel to France and Italy, he obtained secularization from the
Pope in 1808, remaining a priest, but free of the discipline of his
order. He made good use of this liberty, being elected deputy to
the Cortés by the four smaller Canary Islands in 1811. His interest
in his homeland led him to get the capital of the Canaries fixed
in Santa Cruz de Tenerife, and to attempt to create a diocese
of Tenerife. Under the restored Ferdinand VII this liberal cleric
spent from 1815 to 1817 shut in a convent, and it is not surprising that he welcomed the revolution of 1820 and again
became a deputy to the Cortés. Like Sieyès he 'survived', but
only just, dying on 8th September 1823 just before the French-
imposed reaction.

As already indicated, the best approach to Playa Santiago and
La Rajita is still by sea. When I went in search of the boat for
Playa Santiago I was delighted to recognize an old friend: the
skipper with whom I had planned my abortive voyage to Gomera
some weeks earlier, with the same *falua* which I used to see on its
weekly visits to Los Cristianos. He carried me over a now calm
sea, perhaps three hundred yards offshore, past bare cliffs and
headlands broken only at one point by a *barranco* sufficiently deep
to permit some cultivation at its mouth, where a pleasant white
house with arched *loggia* could be seen beyond the bananas.

Playa Santiago is bigger than most Canary fishing villages, for
work is provided not only by a canning factory, but also by a huge
agricultural estate, the *Agrupación Norvega*. Here you will attract
less curious glances, for the people are used to foreigners despite
their isolation. Not only is the estate manager a Dutchman, but its
Norwegian proprietor, Thomas Olsen of the Fred Olsen Line,
lives in a large 'chalet' up in the hills for many months every year,
with children and grandchildren who descend by jeep for day to
day purchases.

They lead a self-contained life up there, and need to. I had had
quite enough of Playa Santiago myself after less than twenty-four

hours, although at the shop-cum-*fonda* where I got a room for 20 pesetas I met a Civil Guard who had once been stationed at Cabo Higuer on the French frontier, and knew all my friends there. But I enjoyed a swim off the stony *playa*, for it was hot in the wide *barranco* where the village lies, as it is anywhere in the islands when the sun is shining and the wind is stilled. By contrast with the south of Tenerife, the south of Gomera is relatively free of wind, due perhaps to the protecting ridges which run up from the coast towards the highlands round La Fortaleza and Alto Garajonay. It is sometimes even called *La Calma*, to distinguish it from the more blustery north.

Playa Santiago is technically a mere hamlet of Alajeró,[1] eight miles into the interior, which although smaller has the *ayuntamiento*. It probably ties with Mogán in the west of Gran Canaria and Garafía in the north of La Palma, as the remotest administrative centre in the Canaries. The youth at the wheel of a dust-covered lorry which rumbled to a halt by the *fonda* told me that it had taken him four hours to travel from Valle Gran Rey, only ten miles away for an energetic crow.

Some of the obscure tracks followed by vehicles like these take one across fascinating if bone-shaking country. There is even a route now from Playa Santiago to the north across the lovely Montes del Cedro with their laurels, their giant heathers, and their ever flowing springs. But the easiest way to reach the north is to return by boat to San Sebastián, and then to take a micro-bus[2] west up the main road out of town.

It is a wonderful drive all the way. But twists and turns, steep climbs and giddy descents, can pall after an hour or two, however

[1] The six administrative 'parishes' of Gomera are San Sebastián, Alajeró, Hermigua, Agulo, Vallehermoso, and Valle Gran Rey. Another quirk of their boundaries ordains that La Rajita on the south coast should belong to Vallehermoso, which also contains Chipude.

[2] The timetable of these varies with the mailboats, the number of people travelling in from the outlying villages, and the mood of the owner/drivers. Enquire not at one café, but at least at three. A patriotic young *gomera* admitted to me—it was humility indeed—that they ordered their transport system better in Hierro. Nor are fares cheap: nine shillings, for example, for the forty odd miles to Valle Gran Rey.

fine the scenery. So that it is the first quarter of the journey that I remember best, the ten miles up that serrated massif, through longer and longer tunnels—though I remember those ten miles in the reverse direction, too, coasting triumphantly back by moonlight to catch the midnight mailboat.

The last tunnel, a third of a mile in length, emerges beyond the divide, near the junction with the forest track across the Montes del Cedro, and the road drops rapidly to Hermigua. Irrigated by the water from the hills, this is the most fertile valley of the island, and as a centre of population almost as important as San Sebastián. For only two miles beyond Hermigua, higher and more attractively situated, stands Aguló, home village of the painter José Aguiar, which dominates a vast seascape with a backdrop of Teide.

An important port, however, could never have developed on this steep and unprotected coastline, which culminates a few miles on in the great pipe-like formations of the Punta de los Organos at the northernmost cape. The road avoids this by climbing again towards the interior, passing the hamlet of Tamargada where, I was assured, lived the descendants of a wrecked Dutch vessel. As it redescends our eyes are held for some miles by a huge monolith, the Roque de Vallehermoso, which stands high above the village of which it has taken the name.

The beauty of the 'beautiful valley' is not typically Canary, but rather, as a *gomero* writer has expressed it, *'una belleza triste de los nortes solitarios'*. Vallehermoso is a mountain village, like San Bartolomé in Gran Canaria or Vilaflor in Tenerife, but shelving away to the north instead of to the south.

I can appreciate its unique flavour, however, with closed eyes. It is the taste of *miel de palma*, the 'palm honey' peculiar to Gomera, of which Vallehermoso has the greatest production. A liquid called *guarapo* is extracted from the heart of the palm tree after sunset, and cooked on a slow fire until it becomes dense and black, relieved by golden reflections. It can then be eaten on bread, with cheese, mixed in *gofio*, or by itself. The natives used to eat it with *gofio*, or with the tarts they used to bake of flour ground from fern-roots. Although its taste is easily acquired it is hard to describe: something between honey and maple syrup, spiced with that indefinable Canary tang of volcanic soils and bottled sunshine which all who have lived there will recognize.

Like all Canary palms, those from which the *guarapo* is extracted are date palms. But at Vallehermoso they produce few dates. There is in fact only one place in the archipelago where dates are in commercial production: fifteen miles further on, over another range of hills, and down into the deep *barranco* of Gomera's far west, whose string of half a dozen hamlets are known collectively as Valle Gran Rey.

Two of these hamlets lie on the low but rocky shore, which has a number of interesting features. From north to south these are the Playa del Inglés, a lonely, sometimes (depending on winds and currents) sandy beach, where English pirates are said to have cast anchor to rest; a small natural pool called the Charco de la Condesa (Countess's Pool); another beach, stony, with a small hotel; a larger pool, called of course the Charco del Conde; and offshore from these that famous rock, the Baja del Secreto, where Hupalupa plotted. From its wide mouth the *barranco* rapidly narrows between its two steep walls. Thanks to their protection there is little wind on the shore except at the exposed Playa del Inglés.

Away from the sea conditions are sub-tropical. I did not myself stay in the hotel on the beach, but in a smaller *fonda* in La Calera, about half-a-mile inland, and the central hamlet of the valley. Every morning I used to climb to the *azotea* and choose a ripe papaw from a tree which rose behind the house. While the proprietress prepared it, peeling it, cutting it into segments, and sprinkling it with sugar, I started on my bread and coffee.

My table was set under a shade to protect me from the already hot sun, and as I gazed out over the banana plantations and the waving palms to the blue sea I wondered if this could really be early April —and 1966. For three meals and a room in this earthly paradise were costing me nine shillings a day! I publish this, against my better judgement, only because Concheta, for whom I developed a great respect and affection, has asked me to send her more visitors.

In the mild evening a small gathering would assemble in the

'street' outside, a street too narrow and irregularly surfaced for the most primitive wheeled traffic. Here with my fellow guest, a contractor over from Santa Cruz on government business, the retired village schoolmaster, and a couple of neighbours, I would listen to the schoolmaster's radio faintly crackling the news from an outside world immeasurably remote.

Then, after we had discussed the latest event in space exploration or Vietnam, I would lead our conversation towards topics of interest less general but perhaps in the final resort more lasting. The murder of the Count would be recounted once again by the descendants of Hupalupa. The prophecy of Aguamuje the seer of Valle Gran Rey, who predicted the conquest, would again be marvelled at. So would the career of his son, Miguan, whose prowess fighting for the Spaniards in Italy earned him the admiring title of King of Arms, so that he was baptized Juan Negrín de Armas. There would be reminiscences, too, of local fiestas, *chasquidos de juerga* as they are known in *gomero* argot, in which the sad *tajaraste* dance is accompanied by monotonous blows on the catskin covered tabor.

Every now and again the quiet of the night outside our little circle would be broken by a shrill note, sometimes piercing and near at hand, sometimes distant and only faintly perceptible. One of the neighbours would listen intently and perhaps comment: 'They want Jaime.' It always provided the opportunity to steer our talk yet again towards the most fascinating subject of all, Gomera's gift to the world, her famous *silbo*.

Other systems of communication by whistling do exist. But Gomera's is unique, according to Professor Classe of Glasgow University, who has taken the trouble to spend several months in the island learning it. For he describes it 'as the only system based, not on prosodic notes, but on purely articulatory notes.'[1] In other words, it is 'whistled Spanish' in which the variations in the pitch and tone of the whistle replace the vibration of the vocal chords.

Perhaps this is why it lacks the easy intelligibility essential to any widely used system. For although whistlers of the same district

[1] André Classe, in *Revista de Historia de Canarias*, Tomo XXV, Año XXXII (1959), page 56.

invariably understand each other, difficulties sometimes arise between those from different parts of the island—between those from the north, for example, and those from San Sebastián.

In San Sebastián itself the *silbo* is in fact heard less and less frequently—although I was astonished to hear it used on one occasion over the loudspeaker of *Santa María de las Nieves* at berth in the harbour. But in the more inaccessible localities it is employed all the time. Cornelius Kriel, the Dutch manager, told me how it helped in running the Olsen estate at Playa Santiago: locating the foreman, for example, or giving instructions when one irrigation channel was to be shut off and another opened. After two or three years there he could understand the occasional whistled word, especially names. But it had its disadvantages, too. He could never make a 'surprise' visit to a distant plantation with a hope of catching the workers unprepared.

In Chipude Jesús Fernández came panting up the *barranco* after being whistled for, and kindly sent and received several messages when he learnt that the demonstration had been put on for my benefit. And in Arure I heard these remarks:

'Is Miguel at home?'

'Yes. I've just heard him whistling.'

And a little later:

'Look at Juanita running up the street. Her father's just whistled her.'

The retired schoolmaster of our evening gatherings was from Valencia, and despite thirty-three years in Valle Gran Rey he did not claim to understand a single word of the *silbo*. But he related this story to illustrate its efficacy.

One night early in his career there the people of La Calera became worried by a number of mysterious lights moving seemingly at random on the steep and treacherous slopes of the mountain at the mouth of the *barranco* to the south. Had a party lost their way in the dark and run into danger? Anywhere else a search party might have set out in grim determination. But a few whistles brought the reassuring reply that the lights belonged to some people in search of a kid to kill for a fiesta on the morrow.

I never asked him where these searchers on the mountain came

23. Gomera: the well-loved Virgin of Guadelupe (p. 154)

24. Gomera: the fifteenth century Torre del Conde, oldest building in the Canaries still intact and in use, rises above the banana plantation which now grows where the waves once lapped up against its walls (pp. 149–153)

25. Hierro: fiesta of the island's patroness, Our Lady of the Kings (p. 169)

26. Hierro: road near San Andrés (p. 171)

27. La Palma: the crater of San Antonio near the southern tip of the island (p. 18

28. La Palma: amongst the pinewoods on the floor of the great central crater, the Caldera de Taburiente (pp. 184–187)

from, but it would not surprise me if they were from Chipude, the village high in the hills behind Valle Gran Rey. Although often referred to as the most 'typical' village in Gomera, if not in all the Canaries, it is not often visited. The tourist finds it difficult to reach during a visit circumscribed by two mailboats. Even the average *gomero* speaks of Chipude in a curious mixture of scorn and awe, much as the Lowland Scot (as in *Rob Roy*) regarded the Highlander in the early eighteenth century. A young man beside the beach of Valle Gran Rey told me that forty years ago the inhabitants of Chipude were wild, and liable to drive intruders away with stones.

'*Pero hoy día están en el siglo veinte*' he concluded with relief. 'But today they are in the twentieth century.'

Our evening gathering was more understanding, for one of the neighbours owned a vineyard up in Chipude, where he had cousins. The day had come to replenish his wine supplies, and he invited me to drive up with him, his brother, and their respective daughters.

It was unquestionably the most 'typically Canary' day I ever spent. We drove up through Arure, leaving on our right the stony mule track which until recently formed the only access to Chipude. When we had climbed as far as the region of giant heather (*erica arborea*, which in structure resembles our own moorland heather, but which can rise to thirty feet) we turned off on to the new road which wound along the hillside for several miles. The first hamlet we reached, El Cercado, was almost as large as Chipude itself, two miles further on. And when we arrived there, I soon realized that the simile with the Highlanders was not mistaken.

They were a friendly but miserably poor people, whose peculiar and once suspect characteristics were the result of isolation, an isolation which had preserved old customs just as it had prevented the adoption of new ones.

Thus at my host's table I ate not only *papas arrugadas*, potatoes in their jackets steamed in salt water, such as might be served anywhere in the Canaries, but also *gofio* spiced with one of the famous *mojos* or sauces of Gomera. This was prepared before my eyes in a *mortera*, a mortar fashioned from a single piece of wood, such as the natives once employed. These are handed down from one generation to another, for once with use they become impregnated with the ingredients, the mortars themselves contribute to the flavour.

> *Come, que me dió mi abuela,*
> *gofio y caldo en la mortera.*
> Eat, what my grandmother gave me,
> *gofio* and broth in the mortar.

I was also able to sample another *gomero* speciality, *almogrote*, a *pâté* made from grated cheese, tomatoes, peppers, and oil.

After lunch, when we went out to the *bodega* to fetch the wine which was the object of our visit, my eyes lighted on a round stone about two feet across, with a small depression in the centre. It might have been one of the Guanche hand mills from the Archaeological Museum in Santa Cruz. But this one had been in everyday use until about three years earlier, when presumably the new road had made it easier to acquire *gofio* from the mechanical *gofio* mill in the town.

Importations from the outside world have fortunately not yet brought to an end the spinning and weaving of wool by hand. Indeed, the women of Chipude turn naturally to this when they are too old to do anything else. Some half-dozen, I was told, were engaged on this most of the time, and in answer to a whistle the nearest old lady emerged from the back of her cottage a hundred yards away, spindle and distaff in hand.

I saw some of the finished products in regular use, and so hard wearing was the closely woven natural oiled wool that they seemed likely to remain so for years ahead. I purchased a *mochila* or shoulder bag, and was shown a *costal* or donkey bag, like those in which most goods were transported around the Canaries until a few years ago. I saw too a great blanket, or *jerga*, and was told the local refrain:

> 'Soy de Chipude,
> traigame jerga,
> si me da frio
> me abrigo en ella.'

Gomera

'I'm from Chipude,
fetch me a rug,
if I get cold
I'll shelter myself in it.'

The good people of Chipude preserve survivals of the past not only in their tools but in their features. They had fairer skins and bluer eyes than their cousins with whom I had driven up, though they were not particularly tall, as the natives are said to have been. Like Highlanders everywhere they are great emigrants. We were greeted by a young man in rawhide boots and a studded belt six inches wide who had just returned home after several years in Venezuela. And many of the able-bodied, men and women alike, had 'gone to the south', meaning the south of Tenerife, for seasonal work on the tomato plantations.

So it was through a largely deserted village that the two girls of our party accompanied me to show me the church, one of the oldest in the island, and far enough beyond to see the strange flat-topped mountain called the Fortaleza. And that was as far as I ever got towards Alto Garajonay, the highest point of Gomera, near which there still survive a few wild pigs, and where there is a perfect example of a *tagóror*, an open space with seats adapted or roughly hewn from surrounding rocks, where native kings once held court in a palace roofed by the firmament.

Driving back from Chipude we were lucky enough to see a shepherd carrying an *astia*, a stout pole about eight feet long. He was kind enough to show me how he used it for vaulting rapidly downhill. This practice, dating like the *silbo* from before the conquest, was developed likewise on account of the difficult terrain.

We stopped again at El Cercado. For it is here, and not at Chipude itself, that the women of five households still produce the same style of pottery that we see in the Canary museums. The clay which they fashion by hand alone, without a potter's wheel, comes from nearby. But the red ochre varnish applied before it is baked has to be fetched from near Alto Garajonay, and is found nowhere else in the island. All ten pieces produced, each with its specialized use, have native names, which seem to have been similar in several of the islands. Four of these vessels, for holding milk, water, *gofio*, and figs, lay carefully wrapped in my *mochila* as I sadly sailed away from Gomera.

Gomera changed very little in the five years after this chapter was written. The population continued to drain away towards Tenerife, where all the development in the province was concentrated. But in the near future the *gomeros* should find all the work they need in their native island. Inevitably the biggest plans are for San Sebastián itself, windy though it is. (It was only on my last visit that I learned *one* of the reasons why Columbus and other early navigators made so much use of its poor harbour. Simply because it was so exposed, their sailing ships never ran the risk of being becalmed there.)

The peace of Valle Gran Rey will be under attack from two directions. For apart from the activities of the ubiquitous speculators, it risks invasion of another kind. I never spoke to a hippie or other member of the 'beat generation' elsewhere in the Islands who did not tell me in a secretive manner that the place to make for next winter was 'the west of La Gomera'.

7

Hierro

The cliffs looked as mysterious as they were sheer, when before dawn one morning I at last gazed on Hierro after a night's passage from La Palma. Was it, I wondered, a subconscious desire which made me invest these steep walls of the furthest, most westerly, and most inaccessible of the Canaries with an imaginary grandeur?

I learnt later that I was guilty of no such lapse. Hierro, simply because it is so small, has an insufficient catchment area to possess a 'network of torrents,' such as in the other islands have opened up the *barrancos* and created beaches. Indeed I could find no beaches worth the name, despite the liberality with which Firestone has splashed *playas* round the coast. Even the staff at the minute Cabildo Insular was vague about the existence of the beaches claimed for the south-east between Taibique and La Restinga.

In this abruptness of its cliffs Hierro resembles Sark—for I have written a book on the Channel Islands and cannot help making an occasional comparison between the two very different archipelagos. One can understand how Béthencourt, on landing, found that he could make no contact with the natives, who had retreated *en masse* to the interior. He eventually persuaded them to descend through the agency of a captive he had brought with him who was the Herreño king's brother. Thereupon, in the most shameful act of his career, which strongly reminds me of the walrus and the carpenters' treatment of the oysters, he promptly carried off the entire people and sold them into slavery.

The depopulation may not have been complete, for later in the fifteenth century we hear of native dissatisfaction with the new rulers. But anthropological evidence corroborates the written record, for there is little indigenous blood in the veins of the present population of Hierro. This may be one reason why *herreño* is the nearest Canary speech to Castilian, with less musical melancholy, and more of the exact enunciation of the *meseta*. But this 'purity' of speech, although easily recognized by another *canario*, is less apparent to the outsider, who will chiefly distinguish the *herreño* for his rough good humour,[1] and for his acceptance of the visitor as a temporary member of the 7,500 strong island family.

In these respects they have much in common with the people of Alderney. And just as Alderney is the only Channel Island with an inland capital, so as it happens is Valverde the only inland capital in the Canaries. 'La Villa', five miles and 2,000 feet above us, seems a capital indeed as we wait expectantly on the quayside for the bus to leave the tiny port of La Estaca, with its twenty cottages and its little chapel of San Telmo. As we climb we are surprised to see below us another group of houses further up the coast.

'That is La Caleta. All those houses are owned by people from La Villa, who go there for the summer.'

A little further on a road zigzags off down to another and slightly bigger 'summer resort,' Tamaduste, with several new houses and a swimming pool. Our expectations of the metropolis rise. (It was near here that the airfield which will put Hierro on the map was being built in 1971.)

We are brought down to earth not so much with a bump as with a dull thud, as we slowly realize that the mean street corner—it is not even a *plaza*—where the *guagua* has set us down is indeed Valverde's centre. These two modest cafés opposite each other are the most sophisticated places of entertainment in the whole island. The two other ancient buses parked alongside form, with our own, its entire transport system.

We are a few feet higher than La Laguna, so that it is often chilly; and there is generally a wind blowing to increase the sense of desolation. Nor is there very much to do, or even to see, to

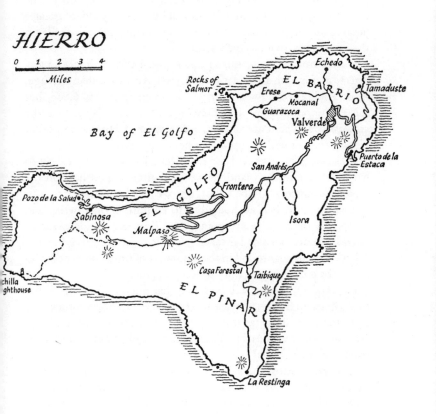

HIERRO

```
0    1    2    3    4
        Miles
```

Rocks of Salmor

Echedo

EL BARRIO

Erese

Tamaduste

Mocanal
Guarazoca

Bay of El Golfo

Valverde

Puerto de la Estaca

San Andrés

EL GOLFO

Frontera

Pozo de la Salud

Sabinosa

EL GOLFO

Malpaso

Isora

Casa Forestal

Taibique

chilla ghthouse

EL PINAR

La Restinga

---

[1] This also applies to the *herreña*. '*Bellas las herreñas no son, pero cariñosas sí!*' as one of them remarked. 'The girls of Hierro may not be beauties but they are affectionate.'

prevent one from slipping into boredom and depression. The church—again like Alderney's—is vast but not very old: of greater interest are the two whitewashed chapels (invariably locked) on the road out of town to the north.

Out of town? One is out of town in just three minutes in any direction, for with a population of 2,500 it is no more than a village. Most guide books give a figure of between 5,000 and 6,000, but this is the population of the *municipio* of which Valverde is the *ayuntamiento*. There are only two *municipios* in Hierro, the other being Frontera with a population of about 2,000.

This administrative division has little relevance when we set to work to explore the island, as we shall after half an hour in the capital. If our stay is to be a short one we may be wiser not to wait even so long as half an hour, but to enquire at once when and where the three buses are going. *Los Transportes de Viajeros del Hierro* operates a splendid service, but it must be utilised to the full if one is to get around in the minimum of time—and there will always be a later opportunity to see Valverde.

On enquiry, then, it will be found that our own bus which has brought us up from La Estaca also runs to El Barrio. Another goes to El Pinar. And the third runs to El Golfo. These, with La Villa, are the four divisions of Hierro which really matter, and their names are well chosen.

El Barrio means 'the suburb'. It consists of the string of small villages to the north and east of Valverde, and roughly on a level with it. The most important are Mocanal, two and a half miles away, Erese a mile further on, and Guarazoca a mile further still. They are easy to reach, and even their churches are serviced by the priest from La Villa (there are only four priests in Hierro).

Life in the 'suburb' lacks most suburban amenities. As elsewhere in Hierro rainwater, when it occasionally descends, is stored in underground tanks, and sometimes has to last for several years. But the villages have the compensation of a glorious view over an immensity of ocean and towards the three other western islands.

Beyond where the road through El Barrio ends there is an almost sheer drop into El Golfo. This cliff, known as El Risco, can be climbed up a steep path by those who know their way: Mrs.

Stone was accompanied up it by guides. It is still in constant use, and one old gentleman, whose home was down in El Golfo, but who owned a parcel of land in El Barrio and had a married daughter there, told me that after a morning spent with her he would return down El Risco on his own. He also told me that his nephew had recently caught on El Risco one of the giant lizards, *Lacerta simonyi*. He had previously believed them extinct since the government had allowed 'foreign experts' to take the last of the ancient species from their traditional asylum on the rocks of Salmor out at sea.

Although I did not try, and would not recommend, the short cut down El Risco, I thoroughly enjoyed another short cut. This was on my way from El Golfo to El Pinar, in the early morning. Had I continued to Valverde I would have had to spend all morning hanging around before catching a connecting bus. So I descended instead where the *pista forestal* from the south joins the main road up on the Cumbre or central plateau.

I set off through laurels. For Hierro, with its highest point, Malpaso, at almost 5,000 feet slightly higher than Gomera's, has just as many 'belts' of forest as her larger neighbour. The mist on the plateau, which alone makes vegetation thereabouts possible,[1] was soon behind me. I was careful not to take the track to the right which passes the chapel of Our Lady of the Kings, the island's patroness, and which acts as the supply road to the lighthouse of Orchilla. Then, after a stretch of open country, began the pines.

It is just not true that one forest of Canary pines is much like another. As I come to each in turn I feel the need for a full page to describe its peculiar flavour, which I then find impossible to capture in words. The *pinar* of Hierro is somehow sunnier than any other: sunnier even, in retrospect, than that of Vilaflor. It is dense enough in places—I got lost for a time—but almost tangibly dry, as might be expected in this dry island, where rain is as rare as in Fuerteventura.[2] The wonder is that it should have survived the hostility not only of nature but of man.

[1] And no doubt also made possible the 'miracle' of El Garoe, a tree whose leaves distilled water until it blew down in 1610.

[2] And like Fuerteventura, Hierro has been 'adopted' by the government and excused much of its tax burden.

Hierro

I was given an example of the latter when I suddenly ran into a herd of sheep and goats. The figure in charge of them expressed great relief that I was not the forest guard.

'To have been found here with my animals would have meant a fine of a thousand pesetas. But what am I to do, when every blade on the bare hillside is dried up?'

It is the same dilemma, so pathetic in the particular, but so sinister in the mass, which over two millennia has destroyed forests from Scotland to Cyprus, and which in this century is taking its toll from the New World and Africa.

Going downhill all the way, I at last reached the *Casa Forestal*, where dwelt the dreaded forest guard. Here, where the trees were beginning to thin, I met a man with a mule, and enquired the distance to Taibique, the main settlement of the district, and itself often called simply 'El Pinar'.

'Only another kilometre. You are not from these parts, I can see. English, you say? Well, I am Juan Fernández, and I have a house down at La Restinga. It hasn't got much furniture, but here is the key. You are welcome to stay down there as long as you please. Foreigners like it down there, and one German even lives down there, and has opened a bar.'

This generous offer illustrates three characteristics of the *herreños*. They are in every sense and the best sense 'unspoilt'. A great many of them possess a second house, or what the French would call a *résidence secondaire*. And they are enormously impressed by La Restinga and their solitary foreign resident.

I did not accept this kind invitation, as I had already decided not to visit La Restinga, the far southern point of the Canaries, about which I already knew all there is to know from a Swiss woman who had spent a week there. She had walked the seven or eight miles, for the only transport is by expensive taxi from Taibique. She described it as a miserably poor fishing village like Playa Blanca in Lanzarote, or Los Abrigos in Tenerife, where swimming was not impossible, but not good either. She, too, was impressed by the enterprising German who has not only started his bar at La Restinga, but also bought up land adjoining one of the putative *playas* on the south-east coast.

Hierro

Taibique itself is a rather larger place, with steep cobbled paths between its solid little houses, the sea far off down a long, long slope, and the hint of something dark and menacing behind. This last, when faced and examined, proves to be merely the pinewoods. Desmond and Dorothy Goode were in Taibique for its *fiesta*, and enjoyed the taste of sucking pig roasted on pine logs. The people of El Pinar are regarded as an independent lot who go their own way, and have a different accent from the other *herreños*—whether more or less like Castilian I could not discover. And here, as at Chipude and Sabinosa, you will see old women spinning in their doorways.

The country west of the track from Taibique to La Restinga is totally uninhabited, except by the lighthouse keepers at the distant *faro* of Orchilla. But it was inhabited in prehistoric times, for a cave near the middle of the south-west coast contains one of the more mysterious of the Canary rock inscriptions, Los Letreros.

Taking the *guagua* from Valverde to El Golfo our route for the first seven miles is the same as for El Pinar. It climbs rapidly from 'La Villa,' and on reaching the plateau passes through a fair-sized village called San Andrés, the only place of any importance which does not fit easily into my four divisions. Soon afterwards the route taken by the bus to Taibique branches off to the left, some miles before the *pista forestal* which I took myself. Then begin the great views.

Better than most place-names, El Golfo explains itself, whether our first association is 'the Gulf of Mexico' or 'the yawning gulf'. For the whole of Hierro probably represents a semi-circular volcanic crater of which the northern half has slipped away into the sea, to give us a steep drop towards a wide curving bay. From above the shore line, continued by the Roques de Salmor out at sea, looks even more semi-circular than it is, and the comparatively flat land behind it is the island's richest agricultural area. Relatively the richest, for this is no Orotava. But a little more soil has collected down there, and the winds blow a little less fiercely. One syndicate, making use of well water,[1] has even managed to cultivate a few

[1] Another syndicate of wealthy agriculturalists from La Palma has recently discovered subterranean reserves of water near La Restinga.

acres of bananas, a small splash of deeper green as we gaze down from the Cumbre.

Good views continue all the way down to Frontera, which proves to be not a single village but a complex of dispersed hamlets, some with obviously native names. If 'Taibique' was not enough to convince you that not all the natives were carried off by Béthencourt, try 'Tigaday' and 'Tejegueste'.

Five miles beyond the last of these hamlets, a thousand feet up the side of a mountain which climbs four times higher, lies the westernmost hamlet in the Canaries, Sabinosa. In remote places at the end of the world[1] time is often described as standing still; and although the church here looks as if it was built yesterday, Mrs. Stone's engraving shows that it looked exactly the same eighty years ago.

So, too, does the famous thermal well just beside the sea, *el Pozo de la Salud*, around which has grown a primitive but extensive *balneario*. I found it difficult to imagine a hundred or more summer visitors filling the cubicles of these rough huts and taking the waters of this inaccessible spa. Its emptiness added a mournful note to this rather beautiful coast, even steeper to the west, and covered by a very Canary selection of 'plants of the foreshore,' which recur to my mind whenever I think of Sabinosa. But there is no melancholy about the taste which I recall: the sustaining *gofio* with rich goat's milk served me by the postmistress in whose clean and welcoming home I slept.

The careful reader, studying a map of Hierro, may complain that I have not mentioned one group of villages above the east coast, halfway between Valverde and El Pinar, of which the most important is Isora. I did not visit them, because I was told that they are not of great interest, and that in fact they have few permanent inhabitants. For small though the island is, and poor, many *herreños*, as indicated earlier, have more than one house. And Isora and its

[1] This was the end of the world until 1492, and a century and a half later Punta Orchilla, beyond the lighthouse, was officially adopted as the meridian by Richelieu. The last and entirely appropriate supporter of this meridian, right up to 1918, was the Austro-Hungarian Empire.

surrounding hamlets evidently consist mainly of *résidences secon-
daires*, to which people go for the summer. Thus, I met a lady who
although illiterate owned *'fincas'* both at Isora and down at Los
Llanillos in El Golfo.

She proved an excellent informant on the present state of the
law of property on Hierro as applied to fig trees. Yes, it was quite
true, she said, that a field was often left to one child, and the fig
tree on it to another. Her own father had owned a field on which
the fig trees were the property of someone else. The grass under
the fig tree belongs to the fig trees' owner—they are low, wide
trees, covering a lot of ground—and many quarrels have started
when the fig leaves have been taken by the landowner for his
animals. Fig leaves have caused trouble in gardens even more
paradisial than the Hesperides, and recent legislation is surely wise
in giving the owner of a field the right to 'buy out' the owner of
the fig trees.

Another village with no true permanent residents is Echedo,
about two and a half miles north of Valverde. Bored by the capital,
in which I had all evening to kick my heels until the departure of
the midnight boat, I wandered out along the road towards El
Barrio. My reverie was interrupted by a greeting from a figure on
a donkey beneath whose wide-brimmed hat grinned a face which
might have belonged to a character in a picaresque novel, or in
Tom Jones. Hearing that I had a few hours to fill, he invited me to
accompany him to Echedo, where he had a *finca*.

A well-preserved sixty-eight, Don Domingo Padrón belonged
to the generation of *canarios* who emigrated not, as today, to
Venezuela, but to Cuba. He had lived there from 1917 to 1932, and
since his return to his native island had become a pillar of society,
being now the head of the *Sindicato de Labradores* (evidently the
National Farmer's Union rather than the Trade Union of the farm
labourers).

Arrived at Echedo, we called on his brother-in-law for a drink
of excellent *herreño* wine, and I learnt that he too had purchased
his comfortable house merely as a *résidence secondaire*. In fact only
one of the twenty or so dwellings of Echedo seemed to be per-

manently occupied, by a retired couple who found life quieter 'out of town'.

A car full of more Echedo householders had now arrived, while Don Domingo himself had disappeared.

'You've been lucky to have met him,' I was told. 'Don Domingo Padrón is the unofficial *alcalde* of Echedo, and he's giving a party tonight.'

By this time another car had bumped towards us over the stony track from town, and in the sunset we all wandered towards his house, where the 'mayor' beckoned me down into a dark *bodega* full of casks from which he was drawing off wine. When we emerged after a long aperitif we found that the womenfolk of the party were busy preparing vegetables and kindling a fire. They handed us some *bocadillos* to keep us going, and we went round to a big room at the back of the house, where to the accompaniment of guitar and *timple* I heard some old *herreño* airs, and an uproarious Cuban ballad rendered by Don Domingo himself.

There seemed to be about thirty people by now, all of whom had come out from La Villa after their day's work. Although I recognized few of the faces, many of them knew me. One man had seen me on the quayside when I arrived. Another had noticed me in the Cabildo Insular. A taxi driver had seen me in Taibique. A young man in shirt sleeves proved to be the barman in the café where I had eaten one of those delicious cheesecakes for which Hierro is famous. I was sad at having to leave for the boat before the deliciously smelling meal was ready, and just when I had located the living heart beneath Valverde's dead surface.

One of Don Domingo's guests that evening was a baker. He very kindly told me the ingredients of the famous cheesecake, the *quesadilla herreña*: One kilo of cheese (ideally goat's cheese, or that mixture of goat's, sheep's and cow's cheese often found in the Canaries), half a kilo of sugar, three eggs, two hundred grams of flour, lemon, and cinnamon.

'But I haven't really given away a secret,' he added, as he said goodbye. 'Even I, when in Tenerife, although I've had all the right ingredients, have never been able to make *quesadilla herreña* as well as in Hierro.'

8

La Palma

Few people have heard of La Palma before visiting the Canaries. Those who have often confuse it with Las Palmas—with every excuse when Palma de Mallorca confounds still further. But few have been in the archipelago for more than a week without becoming curious about this important but little known island to the west, whose fields are greenest, whose women amongst *canarias* are the loveliest, and whose ratio of altitude to area is the highest in the world.

These statements are all true. More subjective is the commonly voiced view that La Palma is the most beautiful island, for tastes in places are more personal even than tastes in female looks. When first I went there I wanted to be charmed and was charmed. Now that I know it better I realize it to be lovelier than I had ever imagined. But now, too, I know the other islands better, and realize that each has a unique personality. La Palma has neither the beaches of Fuerteventura, the dry south of Gran Canaria, the snow-capped peak of Tenerife, the giant heathers of Gomera, the strangeness of Lanzarote, nor the friendly isolation of Hierro. But I am arguing against myself. When pressed I feel bound to admit that La Palma is the most beautiful island of all.

Although only the fifth in size, being slightly smaller than Lanzarote, it is easily the third in population and importance. It always has been. With Tenerife and Gran Canaria it defied conquest for almost a century after Béthencourt. Nor was it merely overlooked by the Spaniards, although only one of their fifteenth-century attempts at conquest has left more than the dimmest memory.

That one, however, will be remembered as long as the Spanish language is spoken. Guillén Peraza, only son of Hernán Peraza 'the Elder' was killed when leading this unsuccessful attack on the chieftain Jedey of the Tajuya region in 1447. Had he lived he might have proved no better a man than his nephew Hernán Peraza 'the Younger', Count of La Gomera and lover of Iballa. But they grow not old who die untimely in the flower of their youth; and those who were left carried 'the body to Lanzarote...' so Abreu Galindo tells us, '... where they chanted *endechas*, funeral laments, of which the memory endures until today.'

> *'Llorad las damas—si Dios os vala:*
> *Guillén Peraza—quedó en La Palma*
> *la flor marchita—de la su cara.*
>
> *No eres Palma,—eres retama;*
> *eres ciprés—de triste rama:*
> *eres desdicha,—desdicha mala.*
>
> *Tus campos rompan—tristes volcanes,*
> *no vean placeres—sino pesares;*
> *cubran tus flores—los arenales.*
>
> *Guillén Peraza—Guillén Peraza*
> *dó está tu escudo?—dó está tu lanza?*
> *Todo lo acaba—la malandanza.'*

The repetition of these lines moves us whether or not we understand them, as does the poetry of García Lorca, imbued with the same fatalistic melancholy.

> 'Guillén Peraza—Guillén Peraza
> where is your shield?—where is your lance?'

There is a suggestion here of the *'neiges d'antan'* apostrophized by François Villon only a year or two later, which reminds us once again that the early Europeans in the Canaries were medieval men, straight from the Hundred Years War or from a Spain still partly ruled by Moslems.

9. La Palma: the town hall of Santa Cruz, dating from the reign of Philip II (p. 179)

10. La Palma: the Hacienda del Cura, an isolated group of farms clinging to one of the walls of the great central crater, which produce the best tobacco in the Canaries (pp. 186–187)

31. La Palma: mysterious rock carvings of the Fuente de la Za (p. 33 and p. 19c

32. La Palma: view of Santa Cruz, the capital (pp. 178–179)

33. La Palma: the monumental porch of the church of El Salvador seen from beneath the portico of the town hall (p. 178)

34. La Palma: Santa Cruz seen from the air, showing the almost perfect crater which closes it in to the south (the south lies to the top of the photograph) (p. 179 and p. 181)

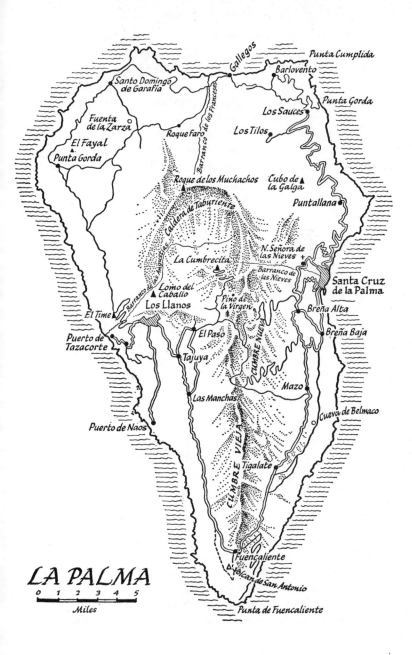

LA PALMA

0 1 2 3 4 5
Miles

La Palma

There is a suggestion, too, of the coming Renaissance desire for youth and for perfection. '*The faded flower—of that his face.*' The idealization of Guillén Peraza in his *Endechas* is a literary achievement comparable with the plastic achievement forty years later of *El Doncel* in Siguenza Cathedral, the statue of a young man killed at twenty-five at the siege of Granada.

It is curious that a dirge sung in remote Teguise in the first half of the fifteenth century should have anything in common with the poetry of Villon or with Renaissance art. It is equally strange that the *tempo canario*, the beat of Canary native music, became popular throughout Europe in the following century. This beat was sometimes of a 5:5 rhythm; and it may be that the *Endechas* were written to be chanted to particular music, and owe to this their curious, haunting metre. Reading them to myself, I automatically and unintentionally adopt the soft, melancholy Canary accent.

Not the beat alone, but the whole background of the *Endechas* is that of the Canaries: *palma, retama, volcanes*. Abreu Galindo tells us that a volcanic explosion occurred in that part of La Palma in the time of Jedey—and it was in the same region of Tajuya that the last eruption in the archipelago took place, as recently as 1949. To the superlatives already heaped on La Palma we must add that she directly caused and inspired the islands' oldest and most exquisite poem.

Big enough to repel invasion five hundred years ago, La Palma is big enough today to have a capital which is more than a big village. Santa Cruz de la Palma—could any name be more confusing?—like the greater Santa Cruz de Tenerife, makes no attempt to turn its back on the port, and has a fine promenade which does much to make up for the lack of beaches. On this promenade stands the government *Parador*, built nearer the traditional Canary style than those at Arrecife, La Cruz de Tejeda, or Las Cañadas, and blending well with the balconied old houses alongside.

This old world flavour is even more pronounced in the narrow main street running parallel to and behind the Avenida Maritima. Half-way along it opens to form a square, dominated by the monumental porch of the parish church of El Salvador. This is an Italian-inspired construction on which work began in 1503, although the church as a whole is clearly baroque. Facing it across the street stands the well-proportioned *ayuntamiento*, dating from the reign of Philip II. Its wide portico has a fine ceiling in heart of pine, and there are more such ceilings inside.

At the very end of this main street, about three quarters of a mile from the port, is a full-sized stone model of the *Santa María*, the ship of Columbus's first voyage, centre of a quinquennial *fiesta* in honour of Nuestra Señora de las Nieves, Our Lady of the Snows. Alongside lies the Barranco de las Nieves, running up towards her sanctuary, and overlooking it from a height on the other side is the Castle of Santa Catalina, a well-sited old fort with the simple chapel of Santa Catalina beyond.

There is more to Santa Cruz than the one main street. Those penetrating inwards and upwards will be rewarded by several quiet old corners, and by one shady square with more animation, where the Santo Domingo monastery has been turned into a school.

La Palma's tourist bureau, occupying a floor of a fine new building opposite the port, is second to none. Its luxurious office is decorated with magnificent 'blown-up' photographs, some of them taken from the air, which clearly reveal the volcanic character of many natural features. Studying them it becomes obvious why the road south must go through a tunnel soon after leaving town. For it has to pass under the wall of a crater.

The free literature distributed by this bureau is technically well-produced and translated into several languages. And the original Spanish really is literature, written by an enthusiast for his island who is also a master of words.

I have been a fan of José F. Hidalgo, a man as noble as his name, since he wrote to me in 1958 when first I was planning to visit the Canaries. At the end of an efficient, factual, point by point reply to my enquiries he unexpectedly took off into pure poetry:

'*La isla es un paraíso; su clima, benigno y sano; sus bosques de pinos y fayas y brezos, preciosos; sus aguas transparentes y puras, no contaminadas y las gentes, católicas, nobles, ilustradas y generosas.*'

'The island is a paradise; its climate, mild and healthy; its woods of pines and beeches (note the old-fashioned use of *fayas* instead of *hayas*) and heathers, exquisite; its waters transparent and pure and unpolluted and its people catholic, honourable, intelligent and generous.'

Even the formula with which he ended the letter after this ringing peroration was transcribed in full: 'Your fond and constant servant who clasps your hand.' An ordinary businessman would have abbreviated this to 's.s.q.e.s.m.'

I had the opportunity of seeing Señor Hidalgo several times. Well into his eighties, he spent many hours every day at the bureau.

In 1971 the bureau had unfortunately been moved to more cramped quarters on the port. More sadly still, Señor Hidalgo was dying.

I learnt that he had acquired his formal, gracious, rather old-fashioned style while on the staff of what was then the greatest newspaper of the Spanish speaking world. *La Prensa* of Buenos Aires had in those days combined the authority of *The Times* with the verve of *Le Figaro*. The pride with which he spoke of his years in its service made me realize that with Peron Argentina lost even more than the punctuality of her trains and the strength of her peso.

With Señor Hidalgo as adviser I planned journeys to cover those areas where I had not penetrated on my earlier visit. But before taking off round the island I must describe a shorter excursion which will lead you to three places of interest in the course of a single morning or afternoon.

I myself started on it before lunch. But then I set off on foot, trudging up the Barranco de las Nieves from where it reaches the shore near the stone model of Columbus's ship. 'Just go on climbing and you cannot miss the sanctuary,' I had been told. And sure enough in due course it came into view high up on the right.

The sixteenth-century church proved to be larger than I had expected, with a well furnished and prosperous air appropriate to the jewelled silver image looking down from the altar, and to the prosperous island which looks to her as *patrona*. And the church proved to be only the greatest among a number of old buildings round a square of which it formed one side. One such building was the priest's house, where with his permission I ate my lunch in the shade of his veranda, finishing it just in time to catch a bus which creaked up the hill from Santa Cruz.

This dropped me three miles further on at the ancient chapel of La Concepción. From there a short road took me to the viewpoint atop the crater wall to the south of the capital, of which we noticed the photograph in the tourist bureau. It was then only a quarter of an hour's walk to Breña Alta, passing below La Palma's simple airport on one of the few flat terraces of this mountainous island.

The valley of Las Breñas is intensively cultivated and settled, and the twin dragon trees for which the village is famous stand in fact some way outside, beside one of the many houses scattered over the countryside. Breña Alta is celebrated, too, for its font where were baptized the conquered natives and the first children born to the conquistadores—presumably by the beautiful *palmeras*. But I searched the church for it in vain. Reconstruction was in progress to treble the building's size by extending two side aisles, each as wide as the nave; and it had probably been locked away for safe keeping. I was even more disappointed not to have seen it when told by another visitor that it was of English origin.

This other visitor was a native of Breña Alta on a trip home from Venezuela, to which many *palmeros* emigrate despite the relative prosperity of their paradisial isle. The extent of this emigration was brought home to me by a notice on the church door. It was a long subscription list of 'sons of Breña Alta' whose donations were paying for the restoration. Against each name was the sum he had given—in bolivares! A note underneath pointed out that these were only a fraction of the parishioners at present in Venezuela, and asked everyone to let their relatives there know about the appeal.

Emigrants' views on Venezuelan politics always interested me. They did not like the democratic President Béthencourt, *canario* though his origins. But of his dictator-predecessor, who took a liberal line on work permits and currency transfers, I heard it said: 'Perez Jiménez era un caballero.'

There are plenty of buses back from the Breñas to Santa Cruz, and several every day right round the south of the island to Los Llanos. Only in the wilder north are communications still difficult. When the track due west from Santa Cruz by a tunnel under the Cumbre Nueva has been modernized,[1] the road south will become of secondary importance.

Even when it does, the visitor should never miss it, if only for the sake of the view of Tenerife, Gomera, and Hierro from the southern tip of the island. Half-way along this road, but some distance below it lies the cave of Belmaco, where mysterious rock inscriptions can be seen. As indicated in Chapter I, these may be little more than 'higher doodling'. But the cave is of interest, too, as the 'palace' of one of La Palma's twelve pre-conquest chieftains.

Even the regular service *guaguas* always halt at Fuencaliente, the pleasant southernmost village where the road turns north again. This gives sufficient time to sample the white wine of this district, produced by the only wine co-operative in the archipelago.

I found it rather too 'volcanic' for my own taste. Little wonder, for half a mile south of Fuencaliente lies the perfect crater of San Antonio, memorial of an eruption in 1677. It seems an unusual situation for a volcano, with the sea only a mile away towards three points of the compass. But a glance at the map reveals that San Antonio is the last and lowest of a whole cordillera of extinct craters running right down the centre of the island. A southern chain called the Cumbre Vieja is continued by the Cumbre Nueva which itself links with the chain of high peaks forming the Caldera de Taburiente, the yawning heart of La Palma.

It is this cordillera which necessitates the thirty-two mile detour to cover the ten miles from Santa Cruz to Los Llanos. Travelling north from Fuencaliente we may well feel that it is worthwhile. There is nothing spectacular, unless we regard as spectacular the glint of the Atlantic a couple of thousand feet below seen through the most essentially Canary specimens of *Pinus canariensis* I know. We are becoming connoisseurs of the species by now, and soon realize that La Palma produces the loveliest pines as well as the loveliest women.

Presently we are made aware of a less happy superlative to which

[1] The tunnel was officially opened in 1971.

it can lay claim: the islands' most recent eruption. This is a source of great pride, and every bus driver will go out of his way to indicate the point above Las Manchas where the gases and molten lava issued from the mountainside, the wide belt of *malpais* which represents the path taken by the lava flow, and the new cape formed during its five weeks' activity, stretching three-quarters of a mile into the sea.

'*Tristes volcanes*' as the *Endechas* chanted as long ago as 1447. *El volcán de San Juan* fortunately caused no loss of life, but several houses and a fair number of *fanegadas*, some of them fertile, were engulfed. Its most serious side effect was to cut the main road, so that traffic between Los Llanos and the capital had to go either by sea, or by mule track over the Cumbre. But for those who were young at the time, 24th June 1949 was a red letter day.

'When we heard that a *volcán* had erupted,' said a man in his forties from the north of the island, 'we set off immediately after work and reached the Roque de los Muchachos soon after midnight. The view was fantastic. We could see flames belching from the volcano mouth, and the lava flow was glowing like a red river. We made the climb several times during the month which followed.'

Until his story made me work it out on the map, I had not realized that it was possible to see Las Manchas from the 7,877 feet peak to which he had climbed, the highest on La Palma. The distance is just over ten miles, but probably five times as much if one attempted to travel it up and down the intervening hills.

One place which would not have been included in his eagle's eye view is Los Llanos de Aridane. Its name means the plains of Aridane, one of the twelve tribal divisions of before the conquest. The *palmeros* are justified in describing it as their Orotava. There is the same old but prosperous town, the same background of wooded mountains, and the same rich fertile valley leading down to a small port.

One of the finest of the old houses in Los Llanos is the Casino. (It always interests me that Spanish towns and villages throw up spontaneously social clubs more lively than those half-hearted community centres promoted at public expense in the suburbs and

New Towns of England.) And the Hotel Time where I had a simple but comfortable room with running water for three shillings a night, concealed a charming galleried patio behind its white-painted lava façade. This looked across to the large parish church, solidly built of the same material.

The church at Tazacorte, four miles and 800 feet below, is older although nothing in the furnishings or the exterior of the little building on a tiled terrace looking over the banana plantations to the sea shows its antiquity. For it was founded by the conquistadores under our old friend Alonso Fernández de Lugo, who in September 1492 landed at Puerto de Tazacorte two miles further down, at sea level. Today this small port with its narrow streets, mean bars, and feckless colourful population of fisherfolk, offers a marked contrast in low life to the sedate prosperity of Los Llanos.

De Lugo had good reasons for choosing it as his point of disembarkation, for the territory of Aridane was friendly to the Spaniards. Psychological warfare had made his task easier. Some months previously a woman born in La Palma, Francisca *la palmera*, had been sent on a 'softening up' mission to her native island. She had returned to Las Palmas accompanied by five of La Palma's kinglets, who were put through a course in Christianity before being sent home.

Nevertheless the conquest was far from being a walkover, although only two out of the twelve chieftaincies offered resistance.

The joint rulers of Tigalate in the south-east, the brothers Jariguo and Garehagua, hated all Spaniards because their sister Guayanfarta had been murdered by a colonist from Hierro. But their territory presented few obstacles to determined attackers, especially when these were supported by a force of natives from Gran Canaria under the leadership of Fernando Guanarteme and Maninidra, two of the most redoubtable opponents of the Spanish invasion of that island ten years earlier.

The other recalcitrant territory, Eceró, was a tougher proposition. It exactly corresponded to the great central crater, the Caldera de Taburiente. Then as now, this only offered two gates in its steep rocky wall: the Barranco de las Angustias which reaches the sea at Puerto de Tazacorte, and the pass of Adamacansis. And its ruler, Tanausú, was just the Leonidas-like figure to defend these Thermopylean approaches to his kingdom.

He was more successful than the Spartans, for he held the enemy hosts at bay not for a single week but for eight long months. And the manner of his eventual defeat was even more shameful. A Melian traitor showed the Persians how to take the Spartans in the rear; but the *palmeros* were never dislodged. Instead, they were tempted down to the plains of Aridane on the specious offer of negotiations. There, on 3rd May 1493, as the pathetic, trusting tribesmen came towards the Spanish camp, they were cut down by harquebus fire. Tanausú, broken-hearted, starved himself to death on the voyage to captivity in Spain.

Something of his spirit must live on, for Eceró is almost as inaccessible today, although no warriors bar our way there. Many will be content with a view down into it. They should take one of the frequent buses to El Paso, a small town a thousand feet above Los Llanos with a factory which produces many of the best *palmero* cigars, and a quiet, civilized little hotel called the Monterrey.

From there one proceeds either by taxi or on foot to a viewpoint called La Cumbrecita eight miles away. For the first two miles the route is not very clear: one must bear sharp left when the simple sanctuary beside the great tree called the Pino de la Virgen comes into view about a mile away at the foot of the Cumbre Nueva. From then on the road is plain, although never straight, twisting and turning upwards through increasingly dense pine forests, with many a botanical surprise underfoot.

The pine forests are still there when one reaches the Cumbrecita at 6,000 feet, and it is over a green carpet of treetops that one gazes down to the floor of the Caldera 5,000 feet below. The wall of the crater opposite rises at some points to almost 8,000 feet, giving a practically sheer drop of some 7,000 feet found nowhere else on earth in this particular formation. An even better view can be obtained by following a footpath to the left which in about ten minutes leads along mountainside and ridge to a more primitive *mirador*, with only the song of the birds to prove one is still in this world.

At the Cumbrecita itself one is reminded of this world by the simple white *Refugio*. There is another such rest house about ten miles south along the chain of the Cumbre Nueva. Enquiry would have to be made at Santa Cruz by anyone seeking permission to use these delightfully sited refuges.

One is always told, too, to make enquiries at Santa Cruz and at Los Llanos before embarking on an expedition into the Caldera itself. Some of the advice may be contradictory, for many who discourse at length on its difficulties and dangers have never attempted it themselves. It is only when actually setting off across the long spur north of Los Llanos, the Lomo del Caballo, that one may be lucky enough to meet someone who has personally visited it, two days or two months ago, and has red-hot tips on the best route to follow.

Here I must declare my own interest. I did not achieve the maximum penetration possible in one day. That was achieved by a friend who walked beside—and sometimes inside—the concrete water gallery into which the main streams of the Caldera have been canalized, following its vertiginous bed high up along the southern wall. This at least prevented her from losing her way, which is the greatest danger in approaching the heart of Tanausú's old kingdom.

Although I got perhaps only half as far, I saw more, and I certainly had a more interesting time. From the ridge of the Lomo del Caballo I zigzagged down to the bed of the Barranco de las Angustias, passing on the way the concrete water gallery, with its cool, swiftly moving current about four feet wide and three feet deep. This canalization accounts for there being so little water in the *barranco* itself. For the Caldera shares with the Montes del Cedro in Gomera the distinction of having natural streams which run all the year round.

Following the *barranco* a mile upstream I struck up a steep mule-track to the left, towards an isolated patchwork of cultivated fields dotted with occasional farmsteads. The sun was hot, and there was little wind in the sheltered valley. It seemed a long time before I came level with even the nearest house, and this proved to be empty and deserted. But before I reached the second I could hear laughter from its vine-shaded terrace, where a big happy family sat about doing various small jobs and drinking wine. Going up to them to ask the way I was invited to have a drink myself, and then further pressed to accept a bowl of goat's milk with *gofio*, and some delicious figs.

I enjoyed not only this unexpected and sustaining nourishment, but also the timeless patriarchal world in which I suddenly found myself. This group of farms, known as the Hacienda del Cura, has a steady prosperity based on the cultivation of a high quality tobacco to which its situation and soil are particularly well-suited. But with a mere mule-track to link them with the outside world, these freeholders express their good fortune not in useless acquisitions but in simple good living which includes hospitality to the very occasional passer-by such as myself. Even the Elizabethan yeoman would seem a vulgarian beside them. They are nearer to Viera y Clavijo's Guanches, with their cheeses, honey and figs.

'Their conversation was neither of gold nor of silver, nor of jewels, nor of the rest of the usual goods dependent on fancy or on faulty judgement. It was rather of rains in due season, of fruitful sowings, of rich pastures, of happy breedings.'

I arose a new man, and following their instructions continued to climb, past the other farms and beyond the last fields to where pine trees took the place of fruit trees, and the red wall of the Caldera towered above me to the left. After some distance more or less on the level I stopped where I had been recommended to have lunch and a rest before turning back.

They could not have advised a better place. There was a tiny water gallery from which I could drink. There were mighty pines for shade. And through my binoculars I was able to explore much of the Caldera's interior, from the point where its two streams meet to its eastern wall, and up to the Cumbrecita above El Paso where I had stood the previous day. I was unable, however, to see the Roque de los Muchachos, hidden by intervening heights, nor the great rock of Idafe, a monolith rising in the heart of the Caldera. Held in awe by the natives, it may well have been the inspiration of Tanausú's valiant defence of Eceró. In compensation, I had a fine view of much of the west coast towards Puerto de Naos.

I had a much better view of this coast the following morning, when I caught the early bus north from Los Llanos. Crossing the Barranco de las Angustias near the chapel of Las Angustias, it groaned slowly up the mountain of Time to a point little short of 2,000 feet above the sea. From here the more distant coastline towards Fuencaliente appeared as a green blur.

'El Time' is not so much a mountain in its own right as a seaward spur of the heights above the Caldera. Indeed the entire north of La Palma above a line from the Barranco de las Angustias to Santa Cruz is simply a steep slope from the crater wall down into the sea. Simply a steep slope? The elements have naturally set to work on this abnormally precipitous island, the highest place of its size in the world. The interior of the Caldera has been formed not only by explosion, but also by erosion. And erosion has been just as active on the outer, seaward facing wall. Deep *barrancos* have been channelled out every mile or two, leaving in between them high spurs like Time from which the water drains swiftly away.

Communications are therefore a nightmare. Mrs. Stone remarked that to travel from one point on the coast to another it was often easiest to climb inland some 7,000 feet and to descend again, avoiding the *barrancos* which made progress so difficult round the circumference. I was soon to realize how right she was.

My *guagua*, after setting down passengers at a series of high-set hamlets, came to a halt soon after 9 a.m. at its terminus at Puntagorda. I had five hours in which to reach Santo Domingo de Garafia, from which another bus would take me back to the capital. (My luggage was already on its way to the same destination via Fuencaliente.) I realized that I had a stiff walk ahead, although the distance as the crow flies is only five miles. But I was unable to find out from anyone in Puntagorda how long it was likely to take, or even which was the best path to follow. Puntagorda evidently communicated south to Los Llanos, while Garafia communicated east towards Santa Cruz, and direct contact between the two was minimal.

'Jeeps do sometimes make the journey now, over the new *pista*' volunteered someone. 'They climb right up over the hills—a long, long way round.'

But my map showed a direct track running much nearer the coast. To my undoing I persisted with my enquiries, until one old man exclaimed:

'Well yes, there's always *el Camino Real.*'

El Camino Real, the Royal Road. The name puzzled me, for I had not yet read the passage in Telesforo Bravo which describes the character of these ancient highways in better words than I can find:

'Even today old folk call it the Royal Road. . . . These paths were traced parallel to the coasts, paved with large stones. . . . In the present day one uses them only occasionally, stumbling on some ancient rambling homestead, or some house, formerly an inn, with the remote atmosphere of other generations. . . . These paths encircled the islands, retaining today the special enchantment of the old and forgotten.'

Early in my journey I passed through the lower end of the great pine forest of El Fayal. Then came the first of the deep *barrancos*, which the path negotiated in perhaps fifteen times the distance required by a direct suspension bridge. There were four such major ravines, and an uncounted number of smaller ones.

Although there was often no one in sight, I was never in a wilderness, every now and again 'stumbling on some ancient rambling homestead, or some house, formerly an inn.' Like the Fosse Way over much of its length, the *Camino Real* had become a route for purely local traffic, and where there were a number of houses this local traffic was still fairly heavy. At one such point I found a group of neighbours at work repairing the surface, but at other points it was so little used that I had difficulty in following it.

Although no wilderness, the beauty of the countryside was a wild beauty: all windy slopes rushing to the sea when I was up, and all airless menace when I was down in the *barrancos*. And ever and anon a lone pine, with the dark forest far above.

It was four hours before the presence of an ancient vehicle beyond a communal wash-house told me that I had rejoined a road. Although in Santa Cruz they refer loosely to this village as Garafia, everyone in the north speaks more precisely of Santo Domingo. Its full name is Santo Domingo de Garafia, for although it has the church and the *ayuntamiento*, it is only one among several hamlets in the territory of Garafia, which like Aridane must correspond to one of La Palma's twelve native kingdoms.

It also possesses a *fonda*, where I had time for a meal, and a chat with two young men and a girl, schoolteachers from Tenerife who had been sent over to this remote corner of the province after their training. I have heard of visitors who spent a happy week or two in this *fonda*, with wonderful walking country all around them— but with no swimming from the high, rocky coast.

At 2 p.m. the *guagua* duly left, climbing far inland to begin with, and passing very close to the Fuente de la Zarza where rock carvings have been discovered. After running for some miles at about 3,000 feet above sea-level it stopped for refreshments at Roque Faro, in the heart of another great pine forest. The beautiful situation and the crisp resin-scented air led me to ask for the rates of the *fonda* where we had our drinks or coffee. They were evasive, however, and when I further enquired of Señor Hidalgo back in Santa Cruz he limited himself to a smile and the comment: 'The *fonda* at Santo Domingo is cheaper.' However, overcharging would be a worthwhile risk for a few nights in this unforgettable north of La Palma, to which I have every intention of returning.

After crawling round the Barranco de los Franceses, longest and deepest of the many ravines we negotiated, our *guagua* trans-shipped us into another which had come up from Santa Cruz. We travelled on, high above Gallegos, and near Barlovento I saw my first bananas growing since Tazacorte. Far below stood the lighthouse at Punta Cumplida.

Presently we stopped for half an hour's rest at Los Sauces, which I already knew from my first visit to the island. It is a big village with plenty of life, with swimming in natural pools beside the sea three miles away, and with pine forests around Los Tilos five miles inland. It is to the springs in these forests that San Andrés y Sauces (to give the district its full name) owes its fertility. But as a result of their efficient canalization the *cascadas* marked on many maps, both at Los Tilos and at the Cubo de la Galga further south, are either sadly reduced in volume or altogether drained away.

The country between San Andrés y Sauces and Puntallana also

owes its prosperity to being far enough from the crater wall to allow, if not quite a coastal plain, at least a certain levelling out, so that the water from the *cascadas* can be put to good use. South of Puntallana the shoreline moves west again, making the gradients steeper. It was along a *corniche* that five hours after leaving Santo Domingo we travelled the last few miles into Santa Cruz, as the sun set over the Caldera.

Canary sunsets are naturally best enjoyed from the west coasts of the islands; and it is back to the west coast of La Palma that I propose to take you for the sunset which will close our last day together in the Hesperides. Half La Palma, from Puntagorda to Fuencaliente, faces the untenanted ocean of Columbus's dreams. Only in the west of Ireland have I seen an equally glorious procession of colours across the evening sky.

Some might argue that other islands offer better views. Hierro, it is true, lies farther west, but its west coast is short and inaccessible. From the eastern five, certainly, there is always the fascination of other islands on the skyline, changing their colour and sometimes, apparently, their distance from us as the sun dips behind them. But in La Palma our imaginations are left free to conjure islands of our own, insubstantial, undiscovered fragments of Atlantis, out of those shifting cloud patterns on the horizon, which sometimes so resemble Hierro as seen from Tenerife, or La Palma as seen from Gran Canaria.

Tazacorte below Los Llanos is as good a place as any from which to watch this sunset, or better still, along the secondary road from there towards the south. We have not wandered more than a few hundred yards between the banana plantations before we come across a cluster of houses which appear on none of the usual maps. A sign tells us its name: San Borondón, a corruption of Saint Brendan, a seventh-century Irish monk who sailed west and was reputed to have discovered a deserted island.

Irish monks did some wonderful things in the seventh century. Even leprechauns were still active. But the legend lingered, to inspire an official expedition in search of the island of San Borondón as recently as 1721. They must have been looking too hard into the sunset.

La Palma

Every day that I was in the Canaries I would listen to the radio while eating my lunch. The world news was followed by the local news, and the local news by a 'letter from our correspondent' in one of the islands. As each island was given an equal crack of the whip, 'our correspondent in Hierro' often had difficulty in filling his five minutes a week. And I felt that he was scraping the bottom of the barrel when he started one day to talk about '*la isla de San Borondón*'. My ears pricked up, however, when he declared that several *herreños* had seen it in 1954, and that as recently as two years previously (in 1964) a single person has sighted it from a point on Hierro 4,000 feet above the sea. It must, I mused, have been a lovely sunset.

And then, thumbing through the *Anuario de Estudios Atlanticos* for 1963, I came across a down to earth article on geology by the practical road engineer Dr. Federico Macau Vilar, which ended on an unexpectedly speculative note, with a wild surmise indeed:

'Finally, in the course of our work, and above all on account of the anomaly presented by the plinth of the compensatory island of La Palma, it seems that it is perfectly feasible to admit the existence, repeatedly ephemeral, of the "undiscovered island" of San Borondón, attributed until now to the fantasy or the imagination of adventurous minds of past centuries, to whom, nevertheless, the theory of the "Compensatory Archipelago" gives, at least in this instance, a vote of confidence.'

This theory of the '*Archipiélago equivalente*' is well argued by him. We must remember too that during the last decade a volcanic island has swiftly risen off Iceland, and another has swiftly risen and as swiftly disappeared off the Azores. Both Iceland and the Azores lie on the same mid-Atlantic seismic crack as do the Canaries.

Extraordinary though it may seem, La Palma in 1971 remained the most unspoiled island in the archipelago. The number of hotel beds had actually dropped over five years from 320 to 300. The runway of the new airport below Mazo was some twenty yards short of the distance required by the direct jets from Europe.

Appendices

1. Getting There

Any travel agency will give details of air and sea 'package tours' to the Canaries, and will supply timetables and fares of the better known airlines and shipping lines. Even the experts are often unaware, however, that three of the most useful Spanish shipping companies have London agents.

The Compañia Trasmediterranea operates services from practically all Spanish peninsular ports (including those on the north coast) to the Canaries, and between the islands themselves. Its London agents are Leinster Lines & Co. Ltd., 44 Leadenhall Street, E.C.3. Its main agent in Spain is Aucona S.A., with head office at Via Layetana 2, Barcelona.

The Compañia Trasatlantica Española operates services from Southampton and the north Spanish ports to South America and Mexico which touch at the Canaries. Its London agents are Lambert Brothers, 88 Leadenhall Street, E.C.3.

The Aznar Line has some half-dozen banana-cum-passenger ships whose names begin with 'Monte'. They offer comfortable and inexpensive passages between London Bridge and the Canaries, Liverpool and the Canaries, and occasionally Dublin and the Canaries. With good reason they are soon fully booked, but the hopeful should make early enquiry at their London agents: Azeta Investment Trust Ltd., Ibex House, Minories, E.C.3.

Few travel agents have even heard of another Spanish shipping line: Compañia Pinillos, Via Layetana 15, Barcelona 3, which can sometimes offer passages between Spain and the Canaries, including some of the smaller islands.

Which brings me to a helpful tip for anyone who wishes to visit as many of the islands as possible. Fares, whether from England or from Spain, are generally 'to the Canaries', with the port of disembarkation unspecified. So choose a line which calls at several of the islands, and only get off at the last.

Thus on my own first visit early in 1960 I took the Compañía Trasmediterranea's slow boat from Barcelona, which called at Tarragona, Valencia, Alicante, Cartegena, Almeria, Malaga, and Ceuta, travelling only by night, and at anchor all day in each port, which I was free to explore. Then on into the Atlantic, to Las Palmas, to Santa Cruz de Tenerife, and at last to Santa Cruz de la Palma, where I disembarked after fifteen days' first-class travel with excellent food. I felt that I had received more than adequate value for £13, but regret that this slow boat, alas, now carries only cargo.

2. Settling There

This book is evidence of my personal enthusiasm for the Canaries. Yet I have no plans for settling there or even for acquiring a house or land there. To those who nourish such plans I would say 'Don't', or would advise them to spend at least six months there before making up their minds.

Many have gone beyond planning in recent years, and their arrival in the islands has caused a steep rise in property values. There have been burnt fingers as well as quick fortunes, and now the day of the land speculator has definitely passed. For the *canarios* themselves have become aware of the riches locked in their own back gardens, and are in a better position than outsiders to spot and to seize outstanding investment opportunities.

Since a private banana plantation with accompanying manor house is now beyond the reach of most pockets, and since almost all other older houses are unsuitable and unattractive, it has become necessary either to build your own villa, or to purchase a ready-made bungalow or flat on one of the development projects or *urbanizaciones*.

If you choose the first course, make quite certain of the title to your land. The Canaries are full of would-be vendors with vague squatters' rights and not a deed to their name. A really capable estate agent, such as Mrs. Caroline Wright of Navarro & Wright in Arrecife, could be invaluable here. Her first year or two in Lanzarote was mainly spent in finding out just who owned what, and in getting permission to sell from the many cousins, scattered over Cuba and Venezuela, who were often joint owners of a single small field.

Remember, too, that harmonization of land law still has some way to go in the Canaries. Not only do systems of tenure differ from island to island, but so, too, does the unit of measure the *fanegada*.

If you choose the second course, make sure that your developer is of sufficient substance to make his project a going concern, with all facilities not merely promised, but laid on. This will be more likely if he has purchased his land from a wealthy Canary land-owner, who will wish to see the development succeed, so that his adjoining estates will appreciate faster in value, and who may even have accepted part payment in shares of the developers. I find it hard to believe, for example, that Don José Tavio would pick a man of straw to develop any of his land in the south of Tenerife.[1]

It is an indication that an *urbanización* is a success if its properties are selling well, even although their price may for that very reason be higher. You will then, also, be able to meet some of your prospective neighbours.

These could be one argument against settling in the Canaries. Even more than many other retirement and tax havens, the islands attract those who do too little and drink too much, and who make no attempt to hide their consequent dissatisfaction with life.

Some of his complaints are justified. The Canaries, however excellent their communications, are quite a long way from anywhere. The absence of many intangibles of European life makes itself felt just as one has learnt to take for granted the cheap food and drink and petrol. Even the perpetual sunshine can pall. At the beginning of May, after enjoying *primavera eterna* since November, I was longing for a real, genuine European spring.

So spend six months there before you make up your mind. You

---

[1] No one saw the potential of this semi-desert more clearly than he, or did more to promote it. Winking at me shrewdly, he commented in 1971: 'I give the great Canary boom another eight years.'

may decide, as I have done, that the Canaries are not for permanent residence. But they will still be there, sunny and welcoming, whenever you feel like going south.

3. Maps

The largest scale is that of the military maps, printed in large sheets which soon wear or tear if used on walks or tours. They have the advantage of showing all the contours, but there are inevitably so many contours in a volcanic landscape that other details are often hard to make out. A better buy for all but the specialist is the Firestone map of the Islas Canarias, which clearly marks all but the least important hamlets, and gives a generally accurate picture of the state of the roads. Although it shows no contours, it does mark the various summits, with their heights, enabling one to judge the gradients likely to be encountered. My only criticisms are that Lanzarote and Fuerteventura are shown on a smaller scale; and that development projects which have hardly risen above ground level are shown as if they were already flourishing settlements. But this at least proves Firestone to be up to date, and you can hardly complain at the price of forty pesetas. This is five pesetas less than five years ago, making it the only article in the Canaries which has actually dropped in price since 1966.

4. Crop History

The present dominance of the banana, and to a lesser extent of the tomato, is a twentieth-century phenomenon. Throughout the Canaries pockets of other crops remain as evidence of earlier prevailing fashions.

The first of these, in the years immediately after the conquest, was sugar. The word *ingenio*, found in so many place-names, means a sugar mill. This succumbed to competition from the New World, and from the mid-sixteenth century was succeeded by wine, the Canary 'sack' beloved of Shakespeare's characters. Here politics helped to destroy the European markets, although North America remained a customer until the mid-eighteenth century.

Two subsidiary crops throughout these years were the *Curchilla* (*Roccella*) for dyes, and the *Barrilla* (*Mesembryanthemum*) for the

European soap and glass industries. In their case the development of artificial substitutes was the culprit, just as it caused the ruin of the third great Canary crop, the dye extracted from the cochineal insect. The nopal cactus, which now seems inseparable from the islands' landscape, was imported specially to nourish this insect, which from 1825 to the mid-1870s made fortunes in a mounting speculative fever which burst with the catastrophic drop in cochineal prices.

Then at the end of the nineteenth century came an attempt at diversification. Coffee, tobacco, and silk made an appearance, and can still be found cultivated on a small scale, as can a more recent introduction, cotton. Potatoes are more important, ranking third in value of exportation after tomatoes. The islands will and do grow almost anything: olives and apples, oranges and lemons.

But 'monoculture' of some exotic product in massive demand in less favoured climates remains the temptation. Today the Canaries are as economically dependent on a single crop as are the 'banana republics' of the Caribbean. Like them, too, they are now busy re-orientating their economy for yet another 'monoculture': that of the growing annual harvest of tourists from the north.

This is the first book on the Canaries not to include a description of the cultivation of the banana. I have omitted it deliberately because I have yet to see one which was readable. I do, however, urge anyone going to the Canaries not to miss the fascinating experience of a visit to a banana plantation.

In compensation I give this anecdote of my visit to Desmond Goode's tomato packing station at Hoya Grande. I asked him why a girl was employed in placing all the small round tomatoes on one conveyor belt, and all the large irregular tomatoes on another.

'Market preference,' said Desmond. 'The small smooth round ones go to England, where they like them like that with their pork pie or cheese roll. The big uneven ones go to France, where they like them like that to slice up for their salads.'

5. Vital Statistics

The population figures which follow are only approximate. The population of Spain as a whole is rising, but the two Canary provinces are ahead of all others in percentage 'demographic growth', so that any census is soon out of date. After only five years I have had to make some upward adjustments in this edition.

Lanzarote, covering 283 square miles, has about 44,000 inhabitants, known as *conejos* (rabbits) of whom about 20,500 live in the capital, Arrecife.

Fuerteventura, covering 788 square miles, has about 19,500 inhabitants, known as *maioreros,* of whom about 7,000 live in the capital, Puerto Rosario.

Gran Canaria, covering 591 square miles, has about 520,000 inhabitants, known as *canarios,* of whom over 270,000 live in the capital, Las Palmas.

Tenerife, covering 795 square miles, has about 505,000 inhabitants, known as *tinerfeños,* or familiarly as *chichereros,* of whom about 185,000 live in the capital, Santa Cruz.

Gomera, covering 148 square miles, has about 25,000 inhabitants, known as *gomeros,* of whom about 7,000 live in the capital, San Sebastián.

Hierro, covering 109 square miles, has about 7,000 inhabitants, known as *herreños,* of whom about 2,500 live in the capital, Valverde.

La Palma, covering 280 square miles, has about 75,000 inhabitants, known as *palmeros,* of whom about 15,000 live in the capital, Santa Cruz de la Palma.

Sources and Bibliography

Le Canarien, the account of Béthencourt's expedition of 1402 by his chaplains Boutier and le Verrier, only existed in manuscript until its publication in Paris in 1630. It was not, therefore, available to the three writers who, independently of each other and for different reasons, wrote about the early history of the islands during the last decade of the sixteenth century.

Del origen y milagros de la santa imagen de Nuestra Señora de la Candelaria by Alonso de Espinosa, a Dominican friar, was published in Seville in 1594, but from internal evidence was already written in 1591.

Historia de la Conquista de las Siete Islas de Canaria was written, probably in the 1590s, by Juan de Abreu Galindo, a Franciscan friar born in Andalusia about 1535. It was first published in London in 1764, in the form of a translation by George Glas, an English merchant and sea captain, as *The history of the discovery and conquest of the Canary Islands, translated from a Spanish manuscript, lately found in the island of Palma*.

Descrittione et Historia del Regno del' isole Canarie gia dette le Fortunate con il parere delle loro fortificatione was written, probably in 1592, by Leonardo Torriani, an Italian born about 1560 who between 1584 and 1593 was the Royal Engineer responsible for inspecting and advising on the fortifications of the Canaries. He liked neither the islands nor their inhabitants, and his historical sections on each island are incidental additions to make his report easier reading: in his own words, '*para amenizarla*'. He spent the last thirty years of his life as chief engineer of Portugal, then attached to the Spanish crown, and until 1940 his work only existed as a single manuscript in the library of Coimbra University.

All three of these were therefore written a full century after the conquest of the major islands, when even the children of the conquistadores and of the defeated had died. Their authors must have had access to earlier sources, and at many points, like the synoptic

Gospels, they seem to reflect the same source, possibly a lost history of the Canary Islands written about 1560 by Doctor (in Laws) Antonio de Troya.

All three, together with *Le Canarien*, have been beautifully edited and published by La Laguna University, which has also brought out a definitive edition of the

Noticias de la Historia General de las Islas Canarias of Viera y Clavijo, first published in Madrid between 1772 and 1783. With the notes accompanying this edition, it remains the great standard history of the Canaries; but three learned reviews, to which contribute all eminent historians and prehistorians of the Canaries, help to fill in gaps and to bring the story up to date:

Revista de Historia de Canarias published by La Laguna University.

El Museo Canario published by the institution of that name in Las Palmas.

Anuario de Estudios Atlanticos.

Everything except history—and a good deal of history, too— is covered by the two volumes of

Geografia General de las Islas Canarias by Telesforo Bravo, published by Goya Ediciones, Santa Cruz de Tenerife, 1954, a concise yet comprehensive work, copiously illustrated, well written, and full of stimulating suggestions.

In English readers will enjoy:

Tenerife and its Six Satellites (published 1887) by Olivia Stone, an intrepid Victorian lady who got everywhere and missed nothing.

The Canary Islands, an Ornithologist's Trips in the Archipelago (published 1922) by D. A. Bannerman, a pleasing account, in slightly *Boy's Own Paper* vein, which by no means limits itself to birds.

Brown's Madeira, Canary Islands, and Azores (many editions, the last in 1932), a detailed, comprehensive guide, which did for the traveller of a generation ago what

Le Guide Bleu—Espagne only does in its most recent editions. It is weak on the smaller islands.

Madeira and the Canary Islands (Third Edition, 1963) by

Sources and Bibliography

A. Gordon-Brown, on the other hand, although intended merely for the 'stop-over' visitors travelling on the Union Castle liners, is a mine of concise and up-to-date information, while even more can be learnt from

The Canary Islands—Mythical, Historical, Present by Yann Evan (published Santa Cruz de Tenerife, 1963).

Madeira and the Canaries (published Hamish Hamilton, 1953) by Elizabeth Nicholas rightly allows more scope to an imagination inspired by the Canary scenery, following thus in the honourable tradition of

The Canary Islands by Florence du Cane (published Adam and Charles Black, 1911), to which Mrs. Nicholas herself pays a graceful tribute. Its watercolour illustrations perfectly capture the older corners of the Canaries as with luck you may still find some of them.

For Tenerife alone the outstanding work, combining readability with scholarship, is

The Book of Tenerife (published Santa Cruz de Tenerife, 1957) by L. D. Cuscoy in collaboration with P. C. Larsen.

Retire into the Sun (published Phoenix, 1961) by Cecil Chisolm reaches a different conclusion from my own (see Appendix 2, 'Settling There'). In his league table of nine 'paradises for retirement' Tenerife wins with 90 per cent, Gran Canaria comes fourth with 75 per cent, while the Isle of Wight and Sussex tie at the bottom of the poll with 48 per cent.

Finally for a good laugh, try:

Canary Island Adventure by Richard Walton, an American adman who took a year's sabbatical from Madison Avenue to relax with his family in Gran Canaria. He eventually penetrated well below the surface of Canary life, thanks to a friendship struck up with a leading Las Palmas family, the Lentons. (He never seems to have realized that they owe their name to their English ancestry: some of the family whom I met one evening at the Cruz de Tejeda told me that although many of them had forgotten English they still retain their dual nationality.)

Index

Index

Index